Foolishness to the Greeks

The Gospel and Western Culture

by

Lesslie Newbigin

WILLIAM B. EERDMANS PUBLISHING COMPANY

Grand Rapids, Michigan

Copyright © 1986 by Wm. B. Eerdmans Publishing Company
255 Jefferson Ave. S.E., Grand Rapids, Mich. 49503

Reprinted 2003

Library of Congress Cataloging-in-Publication Data

Newbigin, Lesslie.
  Foolishness to the Greeks.

  Expanded version of the Warfield Lectures given at Princeton
Theological Seminary, March 1984.
  Includes index.
  1. Christianity and culture—Addresses, essays, lectures.
2. Missions—Addresses, essays, lectures.
I. Title.
BR115.C8N467   1986   261   86-2113

ISBN 0-8028-0176-5 (pbk.)

Contents

Preface   iv

1. POST-ENLIGHTENMENT CULTURE
   AS A MISSIONARY PROBLEM   1

2. PROFILE OF A CULTURE   21

3. THE WORD IN THE WORLD   42

4. WHAT CAN WE KNOW?
   THE DIALOGUE WITH SCIENCE   65

5. WHAT IS TO BE DONE?
   THE DIALOGUE WITH POLITICS   95

6. WHAT MUST WE BE?
   THE CALL TO THE CHURCH   124

Select Bibliography   151

Index   153

Preface

The following chapters are a somewhat expanded version of the Warfield Lectures given at Princeton Theological Seminary in March 1984. I am deeply grateful to Dr. James McCord, then president of the seminary, who did me the honor of inviting me to give these lectures and to President Gillespie and his colleagues on the faculty who received me with the greatest kindness and hospitality.

At the time I received the invitation I had recently written a small pamphlet entitled "The Other Side of 1984," an invitation to the British churches to a more forthright missionary encounter with contemporary British culture, and was much occupied with the resulting discussion. I therefore decided to use this invitation as an opportunity to develop more fully the message of that booklet. This book is the result.

It would be impossible to acknowledge the many debts I owe to friends who have helped me in trying to understand what would be involved by a more explicit missionary encounter with our culture. I hesitate to name any of them lest it might appear that they had some responsibility for my errors. However, I must acknowledge the kindness of Dr. David Ford and Professor Colin Gunton, who read a first draft and made helpful suggestions, and of Dr. Arthur Peacocke, who read Chapter 4 and saved me from one substantial error. The index was prepared by Mrs. Hazel Clawley. And, once again, I must express my debt to Verleigh Cant who, with unfailing skill and patience, converted my illegible writing into lucid type.

Selly Oak
Advent 1985   LESSLIE NEWBIGIN

1. Post-Enlightenment Culture as a Missionary Problem

My purpose in these chapters is to consider what would be involved in a genuinely missionary encounter between the gospel and the culture that is shared by the peoples of Europe and North America, their colonial and cultural off-shoots, and the growing company of educated leaders in the cities of the world—the culture which those of us who share it usually describe as "modern." The phenomenon usually called "modernization," which is being promoted throughout much of the Third World through the university and technical training network, the multinational corporations, and the media, is in fact the co-option of the leadership of those nations into the particular culture that had its origin among the peoples of western Europe. For the moment, and pending closer examination of it, I shall simply refer to it as "modern Western culture."

The angle from which I am approaching the study is that of a foreign missionary. After having spent most of my life as a missionary in India, I was called to teach missiology and then to become a missionary in a typical inner-city area in England. This succession of roles has forced me to ask the question I have posed as the theme of this book: What would be involved in a missionary encounter between the gospel and this whole way of perceiving, thinking, and living that we call "modern Western culture"? There is, of course, nothing new in proposing to discuss the relationship between gospel and culture. We have Richard Niebuhr's classic study of five models of relationship in his book *Christ and Culture*. We have had the massive work of Paul Tillich, who was so much concerned with what he called, in the title of his first public lecture, the "theology of culture." But this work has mainly been done, as far as I know, by theologians who had not had the experience of the cultural frontier, of seeking to transmit the gospel from one culture to a radically different one.

On the other hand, we have had a plethora of studies by missionaries on the theological issues raised by cross-cultural missions. As Western missionaries have shared in the general weakening of confidence in our modern

1

Western culture, they have become more aware of the fact that in their presentation of the gospel they have often confused culturally conditioned perceptions with the substance of the gospel, and thus wrongfully claimed divine authority for the relativities of one culture.

For some on the liberal wing of Protestantism, such as W. E. Hocking, Christian missions were to be almost absorbed into the worldwide spread of Western culture, and this was quite explicit. But those at the opposite end of the spectrum, the conservative evangelicals, were often unaware of the cultural conditioning of their religion and therefore guilty, as many of them now recognize, of confusing the gospel with the values of the American way of life without realizing what they were doing. In the last couple of decades there has been a spate of missionary writings on the problem of *contextualization.* This has been preferred to the terms *indigenization* and *adaptation,* earlier much used by Protestants and Catholics respectively. The weakness of the former was that it tended to relate the Christian message to the traditional cultural forms—forms that belonged to the past and from which young people were turning away under the pervasive influence of "modernization." The effect was to identify the gospel with the conservative elements in society. The weakness of the latter term, *adaptation,* was that it implied that what the missionary brought with him was the pure gospel, which had to be adapted to the receptor culture. It tended to obscure the fact that the gospel as embodied in the missionary's preaching and practice was already an adapted gospel, shaped by his or her own culture. The value of the word *contextualization* is that it suggests the placing of the gospel in the total context of a culture at a particular moment, a moment that is shaped by the past and looks to the future.

The weakness, however, of this whole mass of missiological writing is that while it has sought to explore the problems of contextualization in all the cultures of humankind from China to Peru, it has largely ignored the culture that is the most widespread, powerful, and persuasive among all contemporary cultures—namely, what I have called modern Western culture. Moreover, this neglect is even more serious because it is this culture that, more than almost any other, is proving resistant to the gospel. In great areas of Asia, Africa, and Oceania, the church grows steadily and even spectacularly. But in the areas dominated by modern Western culture (whether in its capitalist or socialist political expression) the church is shrinking and the gospel appears to fall on deaf ears. It would seem, therefore, that there is no higher priority for the research work of missiologists than to ask the question of what would be involved in a genuinely missionary encounter between the gospel and this modern Western culture. Or, to put the matter in a slightly different way, can the experience of missionaries in the cross-cultural transmission of the gospel and the work of theologians who have worked on the question of gospel and culture within the limits of our modern Western culture be usefully brought together to throw light on the central issue I have posed?

Let us begin with some preliminary definitions. By the word *culture* we have to understand the sum total of ways of living developed by a group of human beings and handed on from generation to generation. Central to culture is language. The language of a people provides the means by which they express their way of perceiving things and of coping with them. Around that center one would have to group their visual and musical arts, their technologies, their law, and their social and political organization. And one must also include in culture, and as fundamental to any culture, a set of beliefs, experiences, and practices that seek to grasp and express the ultimate nature of things, that which gives shape and meaning to life, that which claims final loyalty. I am speaking, obviously, about religion. Religion—including the Christian religion—is thus part of culture.

In speaking of "the gospel," I am, of course, referring to the announcement that in the series of events that have their center in the life, ministry, death, and resurrection of Jesus Christ something has happened that alters the total human situation and must therefore call into question every human culture. Now clearly this announcement is itself culturally conditioned. It does not come down from heaven or by the mouth of an angel. The words *Jesus Christ* are the Greek rendering of a Hebrew name and title, *Joshua the Messiah.* They belong to and are part of the culture of one part of the world—the eastern Mediterranean—at one point in history when Greek was the most widespread international language in the lands around the Mediterranean Sea. Neither at the beginning, nor at any subsequent time, is there or can there be a gospel that is not embodied in a culturally conditioned form of words. The idea that one can or could at any time separate out by some process of distillation a pure gospel unadulterated by any cultural accretions is an illusion. It is, in fact, an abandonment of the gospel, for the gospel is about the word made flesh. Every statement of the gospel in words is conditioned by the culture of which those words are a part, and every style of life that claims to embody the truth of the gospel is a culturally conditioned style of life. There can never be a culture-free gospel. Yet the gospel, which is from the beginning to the end embodied in culturally conditioned forms, calls into question all cultures, including the one in which it was originally embodied.

What I hope to do in this book is the following: first, to look in general at the issues raised by the cross-cultural communication of the gospel; second, to examine the essential features of our modern Western culture, including the present signs of its disintegration; third, to face the crucial question of how biblical authority can be a reality for those who are shaped by modern Western culture; fourth, to ask what would be involved in the encounter of the gospel with our culture with respect to the intellectual core of our culture, which is science; fifth, to ask the same question with respect to our politics; and finally, to inquire about the task of the church in bringing about this encounter.

* * *

I begin by looking at what is involved in the cross-cultural communication of the gospel. The New Testament itself, which chronicles the movement of the gospel from its origin in the cultural world of Judaism to its articulation in the language and practice of Greek-speaking Gentile communities, provides us with the models from which to begin. As a starting point, I find it illuminating to consider Paul's speech in the presence of King Agrippa and his court (Acts 26). The cultural setting is that of the cosmopolitan Greek-speaking world of the eastern Roman Empire. Paul is speaking in Greek. But at the decisive point of his story he tells the court that when God spoke to him it was not in Greek but in Hebrew: "I heard a voice speaking to me in the Hebrew language," the language of the home and the heart, the mother tongue. Paul is a citizen of that cosmopolitan Greek-speaking world. But the word that changed the course of his life was spoken in Hebrew, the language of his own native culture.

But—and this is equally important—the word spoken to his heart, while it accepts that language as its vehicle, uses it not to affirm and approve the life that Saul is living but to call it radically into question: "Why do you persecute me?" It is to show him that his most passionate and all-conquering conviction is wrong, that what he thinks is the service of God is fighting against God, that he is required to stop in his tracks, turn around, and renounce the whole direction of his life, to love what he had hated and to cherish what he had sought to destroy.

And—this is my third point—a voice that makes such a demand can only be the voice of the sovereign Lord himself. No one but God has the right and the power to contradict my devotion to God. "Who are you?" is Paul's trembling question. It is the same as Moses' question at the burning bush: "What is your name?" The answer, "I am Jesus," means that from henceforth Saul knows Jesus as simply and absolutely Lord.

We have here, I suggest, a model of what is involved in the communication of the gospel across a cultural frontier. 1) The communication has to be in the language of the receptor culture. It has to be such that it accepts, at least provisionally, the way of understanding things that is embodied in that language; if it does not do so, it will simply be an unmeaning sound that cannot change anything. 2) However, if it is truly the communication of the gospel, it will call radically into question that way of understanding embodied in the language it uses. If it is truly revelation, it will involve contradiction, and call for conversion, for a radical *metanoia,* a U-turn of the mind. 3) Finally, this radical conversion can never be the achievement of any human persuasion, however eloquent. It can only be the work of God. True conversion, therefore, which is the proper end toward which the communication of the gospel looks, can only be a work of God, a kind of miracle—not natural but supernatural.

This pattern is brilliantly exemplified in the Johannine writings. "John" freely uses the language and the thought-forms of the religious world for which he writes. Much of it is suggestive of the sort of world-view that is often very imprecisely called "Gnosticism" and has obvious affinities with Indian thought. For this reason the Fourth Gospel was early suspected of Gnostic tendencies and has later been eagerly welcomed by Hindus as placing Jesus firmly within a typically Indian world-view. Yet "John" uses this language and these thought-forms in such a way as to confront them with a fundamental question and indeed a contradiction. The *logos* is no longer an idea in the mind of the philosopher or the mystic. The *logos* is the man Jesus who went the way from Bethlehem to Calvary. In my own experience I have found that Hindus who begin by welcoming the Fourth Gospel as the one that uses their language and speaks to their hearts end by being horrified when they understand what it is really saying. And so, logically, we move to the third point to which "John" gave equal emphasis: that—as Jesus puts it in the sixth chapter—"No one can come to me unless the Father draws him" (John 6:44). The radical conversion of the heart, the U-turn of the mind which the New Testament calls *metanoia,* can never be the calculable result of correct methods of communication. It is something mysterious for which we can only say that our methods of communication were, at most, among the occasions for the miracle.

The same threefold pattern is exemplified in the experience of a missionary who, nurtured in one culture, seeks to communicate the gospel among people of another culture whose world has been shaped by a vision of the totality of things quite different from that of the Bible. He must first of all struggle to master the language. To begin with, he will think of the words he hears simply as the equivalent of the words he uses in his own tongue and are listed in his dictionary as equivalents. But if he really immerses himself in the talk, the songs and folk tales, and the literature of the people, he will discover that there are no exact equivalents. All the words in any language derive their meaning, their resonance in the minds of those who use them, from a whole world of experience and a whole way of grasping that experience. So there are no exact translations. He has to render the message as best he can, drawing as fully as he can upon the tradition of the people to whom he speaks.

Clearly, he has to find the path between two dangers. On the one hand, he may simply fail to communicate: he uses the words of the language, but in such a way that he sounds like a foreigner; his message is heard as the babblings of a man who really has nothing to say. Or, on the other hand, he may so far succeed in talking the language of his hearers that he is accepted all too easily as a familiar character—a moralist calling for greater purity of conduct or a guru offering a path to the salvation that all human beings want. His message is simply absorbed into the existing world-view and heard as a call to be more pious or better behaved. In the attempt to be "relevant" one may fall into syncretism, and in the effort to avoid syncretism one may become irrelevant.

In spite of these dangers, which so often reduce the effort of the missionary to futility, it can happen that, in the mysterious providence of God, a word spoken comes with the kind of power of the word that was spoken to Saul on the road to Damascus. Perhaps it is as sudden and cataclysmic as that. Or perhaps it is the last piece that suddenly causes the pattern to make sense, the last experience of a long series that tips the scale decisively. However that may be, it causes the hearer to stop, turn around, and go in a new direction, to accept Jesus as his Lord, Guide, and Savior.

The Jesus whom he thus accepts will be the Jesus presented to him by the missionary. It will be Jesus as the missionary perceives him. It is only necessary to look at the visual representation of Jesus in the art of different people through the past eighteen centuries, or to read the lives of Jesus written in the past 150 years, to understand that Jesus is always perceived and can only be perceived through the eyes of a particular culture. Think of the Christ of the Byzantine mosaics, a kind of super Emperor, the Pantocrat; the Christ of the medieval crucifix, a drooping, defeated victim; the Christ of liberal Protestantism, an enlightened, emancipated, successful member of the bourgeoisie; or the Christ of the liberation theologians portrayed in the likeness of Che Guevara. It will inevitably be the Christ of the missionary to whom, in the first instance, the new convert turns and gives his allegiance. This may express itself in the adopting of styles of worship, dress, and behavior copied from the missionary— sometimes to the embarrassment of the latter.

But this will be only the first expression of it. The matter will not stop there, for the new convert will begin to read the Bible for himself. As he does so, he will gain a standpoint from which he can look in a new way both at his own culture and at the message he has received from the missionary. This will not happen suddenly. It is only as the fruit of sustained exposure to the Bible that one begins to see familiar things in a new light. In this light the new convert will both see his own traditional culture in a new way and also observe that there are discrepancies between the picture of Jesus that he (from within his culture) finds in the New Testament and the picture that was communicated by the missionary. From this point on, there are various possible developments. The convert, having realized that much of what he had first accepted from the missionary was shaped by the latter's culture and not solely by the gospel, may in reaction turn back to his own culture and seek, in a sort of hostile reaction to the culture that had invaded his own under the cloak of the gospel, to restate the gospel in terms of his traditional culture. Some of what is called Third World theology has primarily this negative orientation, rather than being primarily directed toward the communication of the gospel to those still inhabiting the traditional culture. What can also happen is that the missionary, and through him the church he represents, can become aware of the element of syncretism in his own Christianity, of the extent to which his culture has been allowed to determine the nature of the gospel he preaches, instead of being brought under judgment by that gospel. If this happens, great possibilities for mutual correction open up. Each side, perceiving Christ through the spectacle of one culture, can help the other to see how much the vision has been blurred or distorted. This kind of mutual correction is at the very heart of the ecumenical movement when it is true to itself.

But even where this mutual correction does begin to take place, it is still—in the modern world—under the shadow of the overwhelming predominance of modern Western culture. All the dialogue is conducted in the languages of western Europe, and this in itself determines its terms. Only those who have had what is called a modern education are equipped to take part in it. That is to say, it is confined to those who have been more or less co-opted into the predominant modern Western culture. Most of the missionary outreach across cultural boundaries still comes from churches that are part of this culture. How, then, can there be a genuine encounter of the gospel with this culture, a culture that has itself sprung from roots in Western Christendom and with which the Western churches have lived in a symbiotic relationship ever since its first dawning? From whence comes the voice that can challenge this culture on its own terms, a voice that speaks its own language and yet confronts it with the authentic figure of the crucified and living Christ so that it is stopped in its tracks and turned back from the way of death? One might think that the vision of the mushroom cloud that has haunted the mind of modern Western people ever since it first appeared over Hiroshima would be enough. But we know that fear does not bring deliverance. From whence can the voice, not of doom but of deliverance, be spoken so that the modern Western world can hear it as the voice of its Savior and Lord?

In starting from the simple model of the role of a missionary in cross-cultural communication of the gospel, I referred to the part played by the Bible. How does or can the Bible function in the confrontation of modern Western culture with the gospel? In the next chapter I have to examine in some depth the nature of this culture that we share, but at this stage it is necessary to anticipate a little. Since the time of the Enlightenment, which—as I shall argue—is the point at which our modern culture emerges into full consciousness of itself, it has been impossible to speak of the Bible simply as the word of God in the way earlier ages did. The Bible has been intensively studied during the past 250 years as part of the cultural history of humankind. We have been taught to recognize its immense diversity, the complexity of the processes through which it came to its present form, and the culturally conditioned character of its views of the world and the human person. If a Christian who is part of modern Western culture says, "I accept Scripture as God's word," it will be seen as a personal decision, one of a number of possible decisions among which those of the Muslim, the Buddhist, the positivist, and many others must be counted, and one that must be supported by arguments a modern person can accept.

Peter Berger is among those who have written extensively about the possibility of Christian affirmation in the context of modern Western culture. In *The Heretical Imperative* he has argued that the distinctive feature of this culture is that there is no generally acknowledged "plausibility structure,"[1] acceptance of which is normally taken for granted without argument, and dissent from which is regarded as heresy, that is, according to the original mean-

1. A "plausibility structure," as Berger uses the term, is a social structure of ideas and practices that create the conditions determining what beliefs are plausible within the society in question.

ing of *hairesis*—choosing for oneself, making one's own personal decision instead of accepting the given tradition. In premodern cultures the heretic was in a minority. In medieval Europe or in contemporary Saudi Arabia, for example, only the rare individual questions the accepted framework of belief. It is just "how things are and have always been." In modern Western culture, so Berger argues, we are all *required* to be heretics, for there is no accepted plausibility structure. With respect to ultimate beliefs, pluralism rules, and thus each individual has to make a personal decision about ultimate questions. In that sense, we are all now subject to the "heretical imperative."

In this situation Berger describes three possibilities for Christian affirmation, which he calls (not very happily) deductive, reductive, and inductive. The first simply selects one of the given traditions and reaffirms it—preferably in such a loud voice that other voices are reduced to silence. Berger takes Karl Barth to be the most notable exponent of this strategy. But, after some respectful remarks about the great Swiss theologian, he finally rules him out of the discussion. Even thirteen volumes of dogmatics are not enough to make your case if you cannot show rational grounds for taking this starting point and not another. It will not do to say simply, "The Bible tells me so," if you cannot give reasons for choosing the Bible rather than the Qur'an, the Gita, or *Das Capital.*

The second, or "reductive" possibility, is typified in the Bultmann program of demythologizing. In this it is fully recognized that the plausibility structure of traditional religious faith simply collapses in the atmosphere of secular urban society. In effect, says Berger, Bultmann takes the mental world of the modern secular man as the criterion of what can be believed. When, in a famous phrase, Bultmann said that "one cannot use electric light and radio, call upon modern medicine in case of illness, and at the same time believe in the world of spirits and miracles of the New Testament," his "man kann nicht" was an unconscious echo of Luther's "ich kann nicht anders"; but the impossibility rested on a totally different perception of ultimate reality. In the end, the reductionist program takes the modern world-view as ultimate and must eventually jettison even those parts of the Christian tradition Bultmann was seeking to safeguard. One does not need Jesus in order to embrace the existentialist's view of life.

Berger opts for the third alternative, which he calls the "inductive." This takes the universal human experience of what Berger has called in another book "signals of transcendence," the religious experience that is the presupposition of all theologies (whether of Barth or Bultmann, or of Muslim, Hindu, or Buddhist) as the clue to the human situation. The paradigmatic figure here is Schleiermacher. The direction in which he pointed is, according to Berger, the only way forward in the conditions of our modern secular world-view. The movement associated with the name of Karl Barth must be regarded as a temporary deviation, and Berger is happy that theology is now returning to the main road. The obvious question is: Among the many signals of transcendence, how does one distinguish the true from the false? Berger answers with the words of al-Ghazali, the Muslim theologian and mystic: they must all be weighed in "the scale of reason."[2] He insists that in giving this answer he is not surrendering to a rationalism in the style of the Enlightenment. He defends what he calls "sober rational assessment" as the only way to distinguish between true and false religious experience; but he does not attempt to describe the criteria for assessment or the basis on which such criteria can be accepted. Perhaps the adjective "sober" has more than ordinary significance, for the original context of al-Ghazali's image of the "scale of reason" is a passage in which he likens the actual religious experience to a kind of drunkenness and goes on to say: "The words of lovers when in a state of drunkenness must be hidden away and not broadcast"; but later "their drunkenness abates and the sovereignty of their reason is restored — and reason is God's scale on earth."[3] This accords

---

2. *The Heretical Imperative,* p. 148.
3. *The Heretical Imperative,* pp. 90-91; Zaehner, *"Mysticism": Sacred and Profane,* pp. 157-58; Ghazali, *Mishkatu 'l-Anwar,* p. 121 (Eng. tr. W. H. T. Gardiner [Lahore 1952], pp. 103, 152).

with Berger's own formulation that religious certainty is located only within the enclave of religious experience itself, and cannot be had—except "precariously in recollection"—in the ordinary life of the world.

It seems clear that the "sober rationality" with which we assess the value of different religious experiences does not belong to the enclave but to the public world outside. It is not a kind of rationality that derives from the religious experience itself but one that judges this experience. And it is not difficult to see that it is in fact the rationality that rests on the assumptions of our culture.

I believe that Berger is correct when, in an earlier part of his book, he takes as fundamental to our modern Western culture the fact that it has enormously enlarged the area in which the individual is free to make his own choices. A vast amount of what earlier ages and other cultures simply accepted as given facts of life are now subject to human decision. With the aid of modern technology, modern man chooses when he will live, to whom he will talk, how he will behave, what style of life he will adopt. He can, if he has successfully mastered the techniques of modern living, change at will his job, his home, his company, and his spouse. The old patterns of belief and behavior that ruled because they were not questioned have largely dissolved. Each person makes his or her own decisions about what to believe and how to behave. It is therefore entirely natural that religion too is drawn into this way of understanding the human situation. It is natural, in a culture controlled by this kind of experience, for religion also to be a matter of personal choice, unconditioned by any superhuman or supernatural authority. We are all in this sense subject to the "heretical imperative."

It is not my purpose at the moment to look critically at the whole way of understanding the world that is expressed in the modern Western culture. I shall do that in the next chapter. My point here is simply this: while Berger correctly shows how the traditional plausibility structures are dissolved by contact with this modern worldview, and while he correctly reminds us that the prevalence and power of this world-view gives no ground for believing it to be true, he does not seem to allow for the fact that it is itself a plausibility structure and functions as such. It is not that there is no socially accepted plausibility structure and thus we make our own choices. This *is* the ruling plausibility structure, and we make our choices within its parameters. It is, if I may anticipate what has to be developed later, the public world of what our culture calls facts, in distinction from the private world of beliefs, opinions, and values. This is the operative plausibility structure of our modern world.

Berger's inductive method of dealing with the phenomenon of religion is itself part of this plausibility structure. His sober rationality in contrast to the inebriation of religious experience is the rationality of this world-view. The public world, which he contrasts with those enclaves where religious certainty is possible, is the world governed by the assumptions of this world-view. The inductive method Berger espouses has been basic to the whole development of the modern scientific world-view from the time of Bacon and Galileo. If, instead of looking at Christianity from the point of view of this scientific world, we look at the scientific world from the point of view of the Christian revelation, we can see that the validity of the inductive method is both real and limited. It is a valid way of coming to the truth because the created world is both rational and contingent—rational as the creation of God, who is light and not darkness, and contingent because it is not an emanation of God but the creation of God, endowed by its Creator with a measure of autonomy. Consequently, through the study of things and happenings in the created world, we can arrive at a true understanding of them. That is the foundation on which all science rests. But this inductive method has a limited validity in that it cannot decide this question: By whom and for what purpose was this whole world created? The answer to that question cannot be reached by any method of induction until history reaches its end, for—short of that point—the full data for an induction are lacking.

Within the world-view of modern Western culture it is perfectly possible and legitimate to insist, as Berger does, that the phenomenon of religious experience should be studied along with all the other facts that are available for information, and that conclusions should be drawn by induction from all these observations. In this way it is perfectly possible and right to challenge a kind of narrow positivism that has sought to deny cultural acceptance to the data of religious experience. Berger is a true follower of Schleiermacher in commending religion to its cultured despisers, and in seeking to show that there is a proper place for religious affirmation within the plausibility structure of the modern scientific world-view. But all of this procedure leaves that world-view unchallenged. The autonomous human being is still in the center—with total freedom of choice. There is nothing that is simply given, which he must accept as the starting point for his inquiry. The whole method of inquiry and discussion simply excludes the possibility that it might actually be the case that the one who created and sustains the entire universe of created beings has personally made himself known at a certain time and place in universal history. Any claim that this has actually happened is simply bracketed with other similar claims to be included in a syllabus for the comparative study of religion. In other words, it has been silenced by co-option into the modern scientific world-view. The gospel is treated as an account of something that happened in one of the enclaves where religious experience took place. It has to be brought out of that private enclosure into the public world to be weighed in the scale of reason along with all the other varieties of religious experience.

I shall argue later that this dichotomy between the private and the public worlds is fundamental to modern Western culture, and that if there is to be an effective missionary encounter of the gospel with this culture, the understanding of this dichotomy is a prime requirement. But at this stage—and with regard to Berger's argument—something must be said. When Berger says that we are all—in Western societies—under the heretical imperative, he is surely right; and yet that statement conceals as much as it explains. What it makes plain is the fact of what is usually called "pluralism." In contrast to traditional societies, modern Western society leaves its members free, within very wide limits, to adopt and hold their own views about what is good and desirable, about what kind of life is to be admired, about what code of ethics should govern one's private life. As a natural extension of this, with the growing presence of large numbers of Muslims, Sikhs, Hindus, and Buddhists in areas formerly designated as Christendom, it is assumed by a large number of Christians that the principle of pluralism applies here also. The rival truth-claims of the different religions are not felt to call for argument and resolution; they are simply part of the mosaic—or perhaps one should say kaleidoscope—of different values that make up the whole pattern. Berger's phrase "the heretical imperative" correctly renders this situation. There is no such thing as orthodoxy in the old sense. We are all heretics in the original sense of the word, that is, we make our own decisions about what to believe. And even orthodoxy (which now has to be called neo-orthodoxy) is just a particular style of heresy.

All this is neatly exposed to view in Berger's phrase. What is concealed, however, is that there *is* a world in which we are not all heretics. There is a world of what are called "facts," as distinct from what are called "values." In the latter world we are all free to choose what we will cherish and what we will neglect; in the world of values the heretical imperative operates. But it does not operate in the world of what our culture calls "facts"; here it is assumed that statements are either true or false. Where statements of alleged fact are in contradiction to one another, we do not simply leave it at that, much less congratulate ourselves on our faithfulness to the principle of pluralism. We argue, experiment, carry out tests, and compare results, until we finally agree on what the facts are; and we expect all reasonable people to accept them. The one who does not accept them is the real heretic. Of course, he will not be burned at the stake, but his views will not be published in the scientific journals or in the university lecture rooms. With respect to what are called "facts" (and I am not pretending to define the word, because to do so will take us much further into the heart of the argument; I am simply using it as it is constantly used in ordinary speech) a statement is either right or wrong, true or false. But with respect to values, and supremely with respect to the religious beliefs on which these values ultimately rest, one does not use this kind of language. Value systems embodied in styles of living are not right or wrong, true or false. They are matters of personal choice. Here the operative principle is pluralism, respect for the freedom of each person to choose the values that he or she will live by.

The way the concept of "facts" functions in our culture is a matter to which we shall have to return in the fourth chapter. It is the centerpiece of the plausibility structure by which our culture seeks to sustain itself. It is, if you like, the center of the temple, the ultimate object of veneration. Berger's use of the word *enclave* to designate that area in which the original religious experience happens is—I think—very suggestive. He interprets the primal religious experiences that lie at the root of the great world religions—the experience of the disciples with Jesus, or the experience of Muhammad on the Night of Glory— as varieties of a single phenomenon called religion, and he asserts that "an investigation of the truth claims of any one of them must be grounded in comparative and historical analysis. Christianity is not an exception to this. It is one of the historically available religious forms, analyzable by the same empirical and phenomenological methods as all the other forms." It follows that "Christian theology cannot occur in a sanctuary that provides immunity from the questions of historical science and of the other empirical disciplines."[4]

Religious experience occurs in the sanctuary, but its claim to truth has to be tested in the public world of facts where scientific disciplines operate. Individual religions may have value for those who prefer them and are to be respected as such. But claims to truth have to be tested in the public world where the principles of modern science

---

4. *The Heretical Imperative*, p. 136.

operate. Here pluralism is not accepted. No question is raised here about the presuppositions upon which these scientific disciplines operate. No place is given to the possibility that what was given in the religious experience could provide an insight into truth that might radically relativize the presuppositions of the scientific disciplines. It is indeed true that Christian theology cannot be done properly without facing the questions raised by modern science and by other world religions. But two things are here simply taken for granted, without argument: first, that the essence of Christianity is the same as that of the other world religions, and second, that all the religions have to submit their truth-claims to the discipline of the scientific method. At this point we are all required to be orthodox with respect to the plausibility structure that is called the modern scientific method. We are not allowed to be heretics. The claim that is massively presented in the Fourth Gospel, that in the man Jesus there was actually present the one who is the Creator and Sustainer and Lord of the entire universe, that he is the light of the world, and that it is only in that light that both the world religions and the whole structure of modern science will ultimately be seen for what they truly are—this belief is excluded. It would not, of course, be labeled heresy. It would have to be called invincible ignorance. But it is nonetheless excluded from the discussion. My concern in these chapters is to ask, How can that claim—in all its winsomeness and awefulness—be heard by this world of which we Western Christians are so much a part?

In this first chapter I have simply tried in a preliminary way to ask what is involved in an encounter of the gospel with modern Western culture. In the next, I want to speak more fully about the nature of this culture. But the argument so far leads directly to one point that should be made now that I have talked about the separation between fact and value. In the next chapter we have to look at the origin of that separation. At this stage it is already clear that the separation corresponds to another division characteristic of our culture: the division between the private world and the public. The public world is the world of facts upon which every intelligent person is expected to agree—or to be capable of being persuaded. Of course, the vast majority of people depend most of the time for most of their information on experts in the various fields. But this dependence implies that we trust the experts to be scrupulously honest and careful in their analysis and testing. It implies that their statements rest on evidence that we could—if we had the time and training—verify for ourselves. Where there are contradictions between alleged facts, we expect that further investigations and discussion will resolve them. In contrast to this is the private world where we are free to follow our own preference regarding personal conduct and lifestyle, provided it does not prevent others from having the same freedom. There are no "right" or "wrong" styles of life. Perhaps the only thing that is really wrong is condemning as wrong the lifestyle of another. In the field of personal values pluralism reigns.

This separation of value from fact is reflected in the separation of private from public life that is one of the characteristics of our culture. And, as I shall argue, the response of the Christian churches—or at least of the Protestant churches—to the challenge of the Enlightenment was to accept the dichotomy and withdraw into the private sector. Having lost the battle to control education, and having been badly battered in its encounter with modern science, Christianity in its Protestant form has largely accepted relegation to the private sector, where it can influence the choice of values by those who take this option. By doing so, it has secured for itself a continuing place, at the cost of surrendering the crucial field. As an option for the private field, as the protagonist for certain values, Christianity can enjoy considerable success. Churches can grow. People can be encouraged, as the posters in General Eisenhower's day used to put it, to "join the church of your choice." All this can happen. And yet the claim, the awesome and winsome claim of Jesus Christ to be alone the Lord of all the world, the light that alone shows the whole of reality as it really is, the life that alone endures forever—this claim is effectively silenced. It remains, for our culture, just one of the varieties of religious experience.

A hundred and forty-three years ago, the great English statesmen W. E. Gladstone wrote these solemn and prophetic words:

> Rome, the mistress of state-craft, and beyond all other nations in the politic employment of religion, added without stint or scruple to her list of gods and goddesses, and consolidated her military empire by a skilful medley of all the religions of the world.
>
> Thus it continued while the worship of the Deity was but a conjecture or a contrivance; but when the rising of the Sun of Righteousness had given reality to the subjective forms of faith, had made actual and solid truth the common inheritance of all men, then the religion of Christ became, unlike other new creeds, an object of jealousy and of cruel persecution, because it would not consent to become a partner in this heterogeneous device, and planted itself upon truth, and not in the quicksand of opinion. . . . Should the Christian faith ever become but one among many co-equal pensioners of a government, it will be a proof that subjective religion has again lost its God-given hold upon objective reality, or when, under the thin shelter of its name, a multitude of discordant schemes shall have been put upon a footing of essential parity, and shall together receive the bounty of the legislature, this will prove that we are once more in a transition-state—that we are travelling back again from the region to which the Gospel brought us, towards that in which it found us.[5]

What Gladstone foretold is essentially what has been happening during the 140 years since he wrote those words. The result is not, as we once imagined, a secular society. It is a pagan society, and its paganism, having been born out of the rejection of Christianity, is far more resistant to the gospel than the pre-Christian paganism with which cross-cultural missions have been familiar. Here, surely, is the most challenging missionary frontier of our time.

---

5. W. E. Gladstone, *The State in its Relation to the Church,* I:124-25; quoted in A. R. Vidler, *The Orb and the Cross,* pp. 142-43.

2. Profile of a Culture

A missionary going to serve in another country is advised to make a thorough study of its culture. When I was preparing to go to India, and during my years there, I spent much time in trying to understand the whole complex of ideas and practices that make up what Western peoples during the past 150 years have called "Hinduism." (*Hinduism* is just as useless or useful a word as *Europeanism* might be in the mouth of a Japanese person summarizing everything thought and said in Europe from Pythagoras to Whitehead.) Obviously, I studied Indian religion and culture with the intellectual tools of a twentieth-century European. But with what tools could I study my own culture? There is a Chinese proverb that says, "If you want a definition of water, don't ask a fish." Indians had no word for "Hinduism" until Europeans imposed it on them. They spoke of *dharma,* which is simply the ultimate principle of how things are and therefore the rule that should govern our lives. Until I had spent many years in India, I was an innocent specimen of modern European culture. I had learned from childhood through school and university how things really are, and it was on this basis that I could begin to understand and evaluate the world of *dharma* under the name of Hinduism. Where shall I find the stance from which I can study Europeanism? On the basis of what perceptions can I evaluate my own perceptions of "how things really are"—perceptions that are part of my mental make-up from childhood?

As a young missionary, I was confident that the critical evaluations I made about Hindu beliefs and practices were securely founded on God's revelation in Christ. As I grew older, I learned to see that they were shaped more than I had realized by my own culture. And I could not have come to this critical stance in relation to my own culture without the experience of living in another, an Indian culture. The assumption of these chapters is that the gospel provides the stance from which all culture is to be evaluated; but the gospel, as I have said, is always embodied in some cultural form. The typical apologetic for Christianity in our Western culture has been one that attempts to "explain" it in the terms of our culture, to show that it is "reasonable" in terms of our ultimate beliefs about how things really are. But what is meant by the word *explain?* We accept something as an explanation when it shows how an unexplained fact fits into the world as we already understand it. Explanation is related to the framework of understanding we inhabit, the firm structure of beliefs we never question, our picture of how things really are. Explanation puts a strange thing into a place where it fits and is no longer strange. Thus it comes about that one person can give a psychological explanation for a political stance and another a political explanation for a theory in psychology. Whether you accept the explanation depends upon the way in which you understand how things really are. What may be an explanation for one is no explanation for another. The question with which I am wrestling in these chapters is this: As people who are part of modern Western culture, with its confidence in the validity of its scientific methods, how can we move from the place where we explain the gospel in terms of our modern scientific world-view to the place where we explain our modern scientific world-view from the point of view of the gospel?

Part of the answer will be to listen to the witness of Christians from other cultures. I shall speak more of this in the last chapter. But we can hardly start here. The difficulty is that most of us are not able to listen to them until they can speak to us in our language. Only those who have been co-opted into our culture by receiving what we call a modern scientific education are able to join in dialogue with us. The others, however charming they may be, however profitable to the tourist industry, are not potential partners in dialogue. They are still candidates — often eager candidates — for what is called "modernization."

A more useful way of starting is to look at the genesis of our modern culture and especially at the decisive point where it becomes fully conscious of itself, the point which those who experienced it called "the Enlightenment." That word is itself a very significant pointer to the nature of the experience that created modern Western culture. It expresses the joy and excitement of those who have seen the day dawn over a dark world, for whom what was obscure and confusing is now clearly seen as it is, for whom the unexplained has been explained—or at least made explicable. It is a conversion word; not, however, the experience of an individual—like the enlightenment of the Buddha—but one of whole peoples. Europe, or at least the community of its thinkers in those decisive years, went through a kind of collective conversion. "We were blind, now we see. The iron grip of dogma has been loosened. The mists of superstition are dissolving in the warmth of the dawning day. Now we see landscape as it really is." If we want to grasp the essential elements in what we call modern Western culture, the best place to begin is with that exhilarating feeling that light has come into the world and banished the darkness, the experience Paul Hazard has called "the crisis of Europe's consciousness."

Of course, like all conversion experiences, this one has a prehistory. It was prepared for by events and movements of thought many centuries before. One could mention especially the ferment introduced into the Western world by the translation of Arabic texts into Latin through which Greek science and metaphysics, and especially the thought of Aristotle, were brought into contact with the Western Christian world. Following this came the rise of the universities, the flood of classical ideas in the Renaissance, the fierce theological and political controversies of the Reformation, the wars of religion, and—above all—the new developments in science associated with the names of Bacon, Galileo, and Newton, and the new method in philosophy opened up by Descartes. However one assesses the role played by all these factors, it is clear that around the middle of the eighteenth century there was a profound and widely shared feeling among thinking people in western Europe that a new age had come, and that its essential nature was "Enlightenment." It was, in fact, a conviction that Europeans now knew the secret of knowledge and therefore the secret of mastery over the world.

What were the elements in the new vision? Central and fundamental was the vision of the nature of reality opened up by science and above all by the work of Isaac Newton. Greek physics had worked with the idea that change and movement in the world of nature are to be explained in terms of purpose. Medieval thought saw divine purpose manifest everywhere in the world of nature. The revelation of that purpose had been given in those events confessed in the church's creed, and thus all study of nature had its place within the framework that the creed articulated. The condition for entry into the world of scholarship was the acceptance of that framework.

The effect of the work of the new scientists, and above all the brilliant vision of Newton, was to replace this explanatory framework with another. The real world disclosed by the work of science was one governed not by purpose but by natural laws of cause and effect. Teleology had no place in physics or astronomy. All the movements of tangible bodies and the changes in the visible world could be explained without reference to purpose and in terms of efficient cause. The rotation of the planets manifested not the perfection of the divine will but the uniform operation of the laws of inertia and gravitation. As the methods of science achieved greater and greater triumphs, both theoretical and practical, the old picture of how things are, the picture derived from the Bible and vividly sketched, for example, in the medieval mystery plays, was replaced by a quite different one. The real world, as distinct from the world of appearances, was a world of material bodies—as vast as the sun or as small as an atom—moving ceaselessly according to unchanging and mathematically stable laws in a fixed and infinite space through time, which moved with unvarying velocity from an infinite past to an infinite future. All causes, therefore, are adequate to the effects they produce, and all things can be in principle adequatcly cxplaincd by thc causes that produce them. To have discovered the cause of something is to have explained it. There is no need to invoke purpose or design as an explanation. There is no place for miracles or divine intervention in providence as categories of explanation. God may be conceived, as in eighteenth-century Deism, as the ultimate author of it all, but one does not need to know the author personally in order to read the book. Nature—the sum total of what exists—is the really real. And the scientist is the priest who can unlock for us the secrets of nature and give us the practical mastery of its workings.

Science, so understood, does not work by deduction either from revelation or from first principles. It works by observation of the phenomena and induction from the results of observation. But it does not simply take the phenomena at their face value, so to speak. It uses the tools of analysis to dissect, separate, and observe each of the elements that constitute the phenomena. This process of analysis has no limit in principle, and any appearance of ultimate unity is a challenge to further analysis. Analysis is followed by reconstruction, and for this mathematics provides the tools. Mathematics enables all reality to be quantified and arranged in a relatively comprehensible structure. What the eighteenth century celebrated as "the geometric spirit" is thus applied to all forms of human knowledge.

The thinkers of the Enlightenment spoke of their age as the age of reason, and by reason they meant essentially those analytical and mathematical powers by which human beings could attain (at least in principle) to a complete understanding of, and thus a full mastery of, nature—of reality in all its forms. Reason, so understood, is sovereign in this enterprise. It cannot bow before any authority other than what it calls the facts. No alleged divine revelation, no tradition however ancient, and no dogma however hallowed has the right to veto its exercise. Immanuel Kant, in answer to the question of what Enlightenment was, used the famous phrase "dare to know." The eighteenth century accepted the challenge, and from that day to the present, even though so much in the philosophy of science has changed, this phrase of Kant has defined the central thrust of our culture.

The challenge is addressed to the rational individual. It implies that the individual has the potential and therefore also the right freely to exercise his reason in the search for reality. This right can only be exercised if other rights are also acknowledged, especially the right to hold private property, since some such property, even if it is only the body and food and shelter to sustain it, is the precondition of any human activity. If no alleged dogma can stand in the way of the right to know, equally no alleged authority can negate the right to life, liberty, and property. The new concept of the "rights of man" comes into the center of the stage. Medieval society was held together by a complex network of reciprocal rights and duties, and the idea of "human rights" in general, apart from this actual web of reciprocal duties and rights, would have been unintelligible. In fact (according to Alasdair MacIntyre), there is no way in which the idea of human rights could have been expressed in classical or medieval Hebrew, Greek, Latin, or Arabic.[1] The idea would have been incomprehensible.

In its earliest form the concept of human rights referred to life, liberty, and property.[2] The most famous and influential statement of the rights of man, however, defines them as the right to life, liberty, and the pursuit of happiness. There is reason to think that what was originally intended was "public happiness," that is to say, the happiness that comes from participating as free men and women in the management of public affairs. In practice, however, the pursuit of happiness without this definition came to be seen as the right of all people. Happiness is, of course, a word with multiple meanings. The question "What is true happiness?" can only be finally answered on the basis of the answer to another question: What is the chief end of man? But the age of reason had banished teleology from its way of understanding the world, and so "happiness" had no definition except what each autonomous individual might give it. Each individual has the right not only to pursue happiness but to define it as he wishes. Moreover, there is a further element of pathos in this idea of the right to the pursuit of happiness. Medieval people believed with great seriousness that final happiness lay on the other side of death. They did not expect it in its fullness on this

1. Alasdair MacIntyre, *After Virtue*, p. 123.
2. Hannah Arendt, *On Revolution*, p. 123.

earth. But the methods of modern science provide no grounds for belief that there is anything beyond death. Hence, the whole freight of human happiness has to be carried in the few short and uncertain years that are allowed to us before death ends it all. The quest for happiness becomes that much more hectic, more fraught with anxiety than it was to the people of the Middle Ages.

There is a further implication of the emergence of the concept of human rights. I have already said that the concept would have been meaningless in an earlier age. "Rights" only exist where there is a legal and social structure that defines them. Anyone can, of course, assert a *need* or express a *wish* apart from such a legal or social structure. But a claim to a right must rest upon some juridical basis. Asserting a right where there is no such basis would be like writing a check on a nonexistent bank. Therefore, if the right of every person to life, liberty, and the pursuit of happiness is asserted, one has to ask, "Who is under obligation to honor the claim?" In the Middle Ages the answer was found within the network of reciprocal rights and duties. The man farming the land had a duty to provide troops to fight his lord's battle and a corresponding right to his lord's protection. Duties and rights were reciprocal. One could not exist without the other, and all were finite. But the quest for happiness is infinite. Who, then, has the infinite duty to honor the infinite claims of every person to the pursuit of happiness? The answer of the eighteenth century, and of those who have followed, is familiar: it is the nation-state. The nation-state replaces the holy church and the holy empire as the centerpiece in the post-Enlightenment ordering of society. Upon it devolves the duty of providing the means for life, liberty, and the pursuit of happiness. And since the pursuit of happiness is endless, the demands upon the state are without limit. If—for modern Western peoples—nature has taken the place of God as the ultimate reality with which we have to deal, the nation-state has taken the place of God as the source to which we look for happiness, health, and welfare.

One further element must be involved in any account

of the conversion experience that ushered in our modern Western world: it concerns its eschatology. The medieval Christian, taught by the Bible, saw as the end to which all history moves, the second coming of Christ, the judgment of living and dead, and the holy city in which all that is pure and true in the public and private life of the nations is gathered up in eternal perfection. This vision of the end is, of course, part and parcel of the teleological view of creation and history, which has the will and purpose of God as its center. The eighteenth century transferred the holy city from another world to this. No longer would it be a gift of God from heaven; it would be the final triumph of the science and skill of the enlightened peoples of the earth. The eighteenth century witnessed the birth of the doctrine of progress, a doctrine that was to rule—with fateful consequences—well into the twentieth century. The emancipation of the human spirit from the pressure of dogma, tradition, and superstition, and the purposeful exercise of the newly liberated powers of human reason would lead to such a growing understanding and a growing mastery that all the evils that enslave men and women would be conquered.

While this expectation was an important element in the exhilaration that marked the pioneers of the Enlightenment, its long-term consequences have been fateful — especially when combined with the expectation vested in the nation-state. If all hope is vested in a future that those now living will not share, and if the nation-state is posited as the guarantee of "rights" that are in principle infinite, it opens the way for the kind of totalitarian ideologies that use the power of the state to extinguish the rights of the living for the sake of the supposed happiness of those yet unborn. And even when this extreme development does not take place, the vesting of all hope in an earthly future means that the relative positions of the young and the old are reversed. The young become the symbols of hope, while the old can be neither objects nor subjects of hope but only an increasingly burdensome embarrassment. The transmission of traditional wisdom in families from the old to the young is replaced by systems of education organized by the state and designed to shape young minds toward the future that is being planned.

In attempting to sketch the broad outlines of the movement of thought that marked the birth of modern Western culture, I have spoken as if it all began in the realm of pure ideas. This, of course, would be a foolish notion. Ideas develop in a context of actual life — political and private. Without opting for either the view that ideas are primary and their political and social consequences secondary, or the view that ideas are merely a by-product of social change, one can accept the fact that there is a reciprocal relationship between them and that one does not truly account for one without attending to both. I have briefly referred to the rise of the nation-state as one of the key factors of the emergence of the post-Enlightenment Western world, and also to the new conception of education as a responsibility of the state. And plainly what we call modern Western culture is much more than a body of ideas. It is a whole way of organizing human life that both rests on and in turn supports and validates the ideas I have been referring to.

For example, analytical and mathematical reason is not content to deal with physics or astronomy; it must extend its operation to human behavior, work, and society. The work of the traditional craftsman that spanned the whole process from raw material to finished product is analyzed into its smallest parts and then broken up into separate operations, each given over to a different workman. By this division of labor, it is possible to increase enormously the quantity of finished articles produced, but the individual worker no longer shares directly in the vision of the final product that governs the whole process. His work is assimilated more and more into the repetitive action of a machine rather than to the purposeful work of the craftsman, whose operations are all governed by a vision of the end. Craftsmanship is replaced by labor, and human work is assimilated into the pattern of the Newtonian universe, from which teleology is banished. The individual worker, for example, does not know whether his product is going to make a family car or a fighter plane.

Hannah Arendt, in her profound study *The Human Condition,* divides human activity into labor, work, and action. Labor is "the activity which corresponds to the biological process of the human body"; it is "man's metabolism with nature" (Marx). It is the cyclical process that has to be repeated endlessly if life is to continue. It leaves nothing enduring behind. Work is the activity that transcends the merely biological character of human existence. It looks to the creation of something that will endure in the world of things after the worker is dead—an artifact, a poem, a system of laws. Work creates a world that outlasts the individual. Action, on the other hand, is the activity that goes on in the mutual interaction of human beings. It arises from the fact that human beings are different from one another, and finds expression in the shared life of a society.[3] The effect of the post-Enlightenment project for human society is that all human activity is absorbed into labor. It becomes an unending cycle of production for the sake of consumption. The modern conception of "built-in obsolescence" makes this clear. The cycle of production and consumption has to be kept going, and the work of the artist or craftsman who aims to create something enduring becomes marginal to the economic order. Likewise, the world of action, of politics, is reduced to a conflict of views about how to keep the cycle of production and consumption going. Questions of ultimate purpose are excluded from the public world.

The division of labor has as a further consequence the growth of a market economy. In an earlier age, as in contemporary premodern societies, farming and the various skilled crafts were mainly for the use of the family or the local community. The market in which money operated as a means of exchange was only a minor and marginal part of the economy. But as the principle of the division of labor gained ascendancy, the market moved into the central place as the mechanism that linked all the separate procedures with each other and with the consumers. The modern science of economics was born. Once again teleology was removed, because economics was no

---

3. Hannah Arendt, *The Human Condition,* pp. 7ff.

longer part of ethics. It was not concerned with the purpose of human life. It was no longer about the requirements of justice and the dangers of covetousness. It became the science of the working of the market as a self-operating mechanism modeled on the Newtonian universe. The difference was that the fundamental law governing its movements, corresponding to the law of gravitation in Newton, is the law of covetousness assumed as the basic drive of human nature. What does not enter the market is ignored. Gross National Product refers only to what enters the market. It excludes the work of the housewife, of the gardener growing his own food. It includes the operations of the gambling syndicate, the arms salesman, and the drug pusher.

Two further consequences follow. One is the removal of work from the home to the factory, with immense consequences for the nature of society. The home is no longer the place of work, and the family is no longer the working unit. The way is opened for a deep divide between the public world of work, of exchange, of economics, and the private world that is withdrawn from the world of work and remains under another vision of how things are. In the public world the workers in the factory are related to each other anonymously as units in a mechanical process. They are replaceable parts. They may not even know each other's names. In the home people are known to one another as irreplaceable persons, and their mutual understanding as persons is what constitutes the home. Moreover (at least during the first 150 years of the Industrial Revolution), it was the men who operated the public world of the factory and the market, and the women who were relegated to the private sector. The fissure in society divided the sexes: the man dealt with public facts, the woman with personal values. The man was the producer, the woman the consumer (even though, in fact, she worked as long and as hard in the home as her man worked in the office or the factory). Today's feminism, which is characteristic of modern—as distinct from traditional—societies, represents in part the revolt of women against these distortions.

A second consequence of the mechanization of work was the growth of huge cities. Urbanization is one of the most obvious visible symptoms of what is called modernization. Before the harnessing of electrical power and the recent developments in electronics, division and mechanization of labor required the concentration of workers in factories, and of factories in cities where goods could easily be moved from one stage of production to the next. Urbanization breaks up traditional family-based communities and introduces people into a world where there is a multiplicity of human networks, each controlled by different purposes. In traditional rural societies, each person is securely fixed in a single human milieu that embraces work, leisure, family relationships, and religion. These all form part of a given world that is accepted as real and within which the individual person has a secure and well-defined identity. In a city the individual is in the presence of multiple possibilities. His neighbors— perhaps in a multistory apartment—may all have their work in different parts of the city, and he has no necessary relationship with them. Each one has a variety of possible networks with which he can decide to connect or not to connect; he is in the midst of a plurality of worlds among which he chooses. And to that extent his identity is a matter for his own choice, and so for anxiety and doubt. In the milling crowds of the city, composed of individuals each pursuing goals of his or her own choice, the individual's sense of being in a world without landmarks is heightened—sometimes to the point of despair.

The division and mechanization of labor, the development of a market economy, the dichotomy of private and public worlds, and the growth of big cities— these are all key characteristics of modern culture that are not found in the premodern cultures of Asia and Africa, except insofar as those cultures have succumbed to "modernization." They rest upon and in turn reinforce the new view of the human individual that marked the birth of the modern world at the Enlightenment. One further stroke must be added to this rough sketch of the public aspects of our culture. Many observers have noted that bureaucratization plays a central role in modern societies. The division of labor and the consequent pluralization and complexification of society require the development of techniques for large-scale control. Bureaucracy applies the mechanical model to this task. It provides machinery in which there is a high degree of division of labor, of specialization, of predictability, and of anonymity. It is of the essence of bureaucracy that it sets out to achieve a kind of justice by treating each individual as an anonymous and replaceable unit. The introduction into bureaucratic procedures of the personal relationships that govern the private life of the home is—in bureaucratic terms—corruption and nepotism. Bureaucracy applies the principles of reason as understood at the Enlightenment to human life in the public sphere: the analysis of every situation into the smallest possible components and the recombination of these elements in terms of logical relationships which, ideally, can be expressed in mathematical terms and handled by a computer. In its ultimate development, bureaucracy is the rule of nobody and is therefore experienced as tyranny. The attempt to interpret human behavior in terms of models derived from the natural sciences eventually destroys personal responsibility. Action—in the sense in which Hannah Arendt uses the word—is absorbed along with work into labor. It becomes part of the cycle of production and consumption. While the growth of huge cities in the early decades of the modern age was mainly due to the growth of the factories and their power-based mechanization, the contemporary growth in the cities is more largely attributable to bureaucratization. The typical new building in a modern city is a block of offices.

I have tried in a few strokes to sketch what seem to me to be the essential features of our culture, first by looking at the manner in which the thinkers of the Enlightenment expressed their new way of understanding the world, and then at the manners in which these have been embodied in the life of modern Western societies. By this arrangement of material, I must repeat, I am not implying a one-way, cause-and-effect relationship between ideas and social and industrial realities. Hannah Arendt has argued that the invention of the telescope was among the most fundamental causes of the emergence of the modern mind because it showed that the world is not what it appears to be and thus led directly to Cartesian doubt and to the attempt to found all certainty upon the experience that the conscious self has of its own thinking processes.[4] It can also be argued that one of the powerful sources of the new thinking of the Enlightenment was the opening of new horizons and the discovery of new cultures through the long voyages of the sixteenth and subsequent centuries, which were made possible by improved instruments for navigation. And certainly there is a reciprocal influence (as I have argued) of the growth of factories, cities, and the market economy on the way people understand human life. But we shall not be wrong, I think, if we take the abandonment of teleology as the key to the understanding of nature for our primary clue to understanding the whole of these vast changes in the human situation. I shall argue that this is what underlies that decisive feature of our culture that can be described both as the division of human life into public and private, and as the separation of fact and value.

Let us look at the central fact, the elimination of teleology. It is difficult to describe human behaviors without using the category of purpose. While it is, of course, possible to describe what a lecturer is doing in terms of the cause-and-effect nexus between electrical impulses in the cerebral cortex, chemical changes in the muscles, and sound waves in the air of the room, and while this description could in principle be exhaustive, no intelligent person would accept it as the explanation of what was happening. An explanation would have to express the purpose of the speaker to communicate some vision of reality to the hearers. Passing from human behavior to biology in general, while it seems natural to explain the behavior of an animal in terms of purpose, a plausible case can be made for explaining at least some of it without that category. But when we move on to chemistry, physics, and astrono-

---

4. Ibid., pp. 257ff.

my, it seems obvious, at least to the modern Western mind, that explanation must be in terms of cause and effect, without recourse to teleology. Greek science, as we have seen, did take purpose as a category of explanation in physics. Motion was seen as inexplicable unless it was purposive—a movement from the less good to the good. From the point of view of modern science, that was a blind alley. The breakthrough in the sixteenth and seventeenth centuries that gave birth to modern science would have been impossible without the methodological elimination of the idea of purpose from the study of physics and astronomy. The enormous achievements that have followed have had the effect of converting (in the minds of very many) this methodological elimination into a disposition to believe that purpose has no place as a category of explanation in any exercise that claims to be "scientific," and thus to look for the explanation of everything, including both animal and human behavior, without reference to purpose. The result has been the creation of the mental world with which we are so familiar—a world in which everything will ultimately be explained as the effect of antecedent causes that operate with the precision and the predictability of the Newtonian atoms, and in which no alleged knowledge is regarded secure against doubt unless it conforms to this pattern.

And yet purpose remains an inescapable element in human life. Human beings do entertain purposes and set out to achieve them. The immense achievements of modern science themselves are, very obviously, the outcome of the purposeful efforts of hundreds of thousands of men and women dedicated to the achievement of something that is valuable—a true understanding of how things are. A strange fissure thus runs right through the consciousness of modern Western man. The ideal that he seeks would eliminate all ideals. With dedicated zeal he purposes to explain the world as something that is without purpose. And, as I have suggested, this fissure becomes visible in two ways: in the dichotomy (one of the outstanding marks of a "modern" society) between the public and the private worlds, and in the dichotomy in thought between what are commonly called "facts" and what are called "values." The public world is a world of facts that are the same for everyone, whatever his values may be; the private world is a world of values where all are free to choose their own values and therefore to pursue such courses of action as will correspond with them.

At the intellectual level, this fissure expresses itself in the search for "value-free" facts, and for a science of human behavior that shall be "objective" in the sense that no value judgments are allowed to have a place in its operations. Language has to be "purified" so that any suggestion of purpose is removed in order to achieve a "scientific" theory of how societies function. This kind of allegedly scientific sociology is so far from the experience of human life as it is lived that it is perhaps destined to remain marginal in any society that could survive. But the ideal that it embodies—an ideal that one might define paradoxically by saying that the only really valuable things are value-free facts—has enormous power in the public life of modern societies.

Thinkers of the Enlightenment asked how it could be possible to move logically from a statement of fact ("this is so") to a judgment of value ("this ought to be approved or done"). Because—in the terms of post-Enlightenment thought—there could be no logically viable move from "is" to "ought," the past 250 years have seen numerous attempts to find a basis for moral judgments somewhere else. Alasdair MacIntyre has described these attempts and shown how, in every case, the moral judgments for which a basis was sought were in fact survivals from the pre-Enlightenment thought-world.[5] It is not surprising that the attempt failed. It was an attempt to base a traditional morality on a new and different view of what is the case. No moral law of universal validity can be founded upon the view of what-is-the-case that post-Enlightenment science taught people to hold. If the world is as post-Enlightenment thought understood it to be, then it is not logically possible to move from a statement in the form "this is the case" to a statement in the form "this ought to be done."

Yet, as MacIntyre points out, the view that no sentence

5. MacIntyre, *After Virtue,* pp. 35–59.

with the verb "ought" can logically follow from a sentence with the verb "is" rests on the assumption that statements of fact do not include statements of purpose.[6] From the factual statement "this watch has lost only five seconds in two years," it is proper to move to a judgment of value: "this is a good watch"; provided—and only provided—that the word "watch" defines an object whose purpose is to keep time and not a collection of pieces of metal to be used for any purpose its owner as a private person may care to entertain, such as decorating the living room or throwing at the cat. Thus, if it is true that the whole world of observable phenomena, including not only the inanimate world and the world of subhuman life but also the life of human societies, is to be truly understood only in terms of networks of cause and effect and that the idea of purpose must be excluded from any truly scientific account of the facts, then it is quite certain that there is no way in which any system of values can be founded upon the facts so understood. The fissure cannot be healed. If purpose is not a feature of the world of "facts," and if human beings entertain purposes, that is their personal choice and they will have to create these purposes for themselves. Their purposes have no authority beyond the strength of conviction with which they hold them. These purposes cannot claim the authority of facts: they are personal opinions, and those who hold them can do so, provided they do not interfere with the freedom of others to hold different opinions. But they can claim no universal authority; they belong to the private world.

As I have already pointed out, one of the most influential statements of what this implies, affirmed as an axiom that is self-evident, is that every human being has an equal right to the pursuit of happiness. What this affirms is the right to the pursuit of happiness, not to the pursuit of the end for which humans, as a matter of fact, exist. Happiness is to be defined by each individual in his own way. There is no given, factual, objective standard by which different ideas of happiness might be tested to see whether they conform to reality or spring from illusion.

---

6. Ibid., p. 55.

The hard question—true or false—applies to the world of fact, and on this all sane people are expected to agree. On the question of good or bad, there is no such objective standard. A scientific understanding of the world of phenomena must exclude the idea that there is a given purpose running through all things, about which one may be in the truth or in error.

One area in which the fissure becomes very perceptible is in the field of education. Modern post-Enlightenment societies have, as an essential part of their development, set up public educational systems by which children are taken away from their parents and introduced to those areas of knowledge and skill that enable them to function effectively in the public world of facts. Science is taught as a true account of how things really are. But what can be done about values? On what basis are they to be taught? Values in any culture, insofar as they are consciously and reflectively affirmed and not merely embodied in customary behavior, are based on some vision of the ultimate nature of things. In effect, they have traditionally been rooted in religion. The modern scientific view does not provide a basis, for it excludes purpose as a factor in the ultimate constitution of things. That the development of the individual person is governed by the program encoded in the DNA molecule is a fact every educated person is expected to know and accept. It will be part of the curriculum in the public school system. That every human being is made to glorify God and enjoy him forever is an opinion held by some people but not part of public truth. Yet, if it is true, it is at least as important as anything else in the preparation of young people for their journey through life.

How is this fissure between public truth and private opinion to be dealt with? Should religion be excluded from the public schools, as it is in the United States, or laid down as one of the compulsory subjects, as it is in the United Kingdom? In other words, should the fissure appear within the school curriculum or between the school and the home? I do not venture to speak of the American experience, but the recent British experience is instructive. Up to about 1960, "religious education" in British schools was based on the Bible. But, if we may speak in general terms, the contradiction between what was taught in "religious education" and what was communicated in the rest of the curriculum was such that, for the vast majority of the products of the schools, Christianity remained a rejected option for the rest of their lives. Since 1960, British schools have had to accommodate a large number—sometimes a majority—of children from Muslim, Hindu, Sikh, and Buddhist homes. Since that date, and predominantly now, "religious education" in British schools has increasingly been an introduction to some or all of these religions with the invitation to the student to take his choice from the well-furnished shelves of this ideological supermarket. In the physics classroom the student learns what the "facts" are and is expected at the end to believe the truth of what he has learned. In the religious education classroom he is invited to choose what he likes best. It is not surprising that the goods that are most often picked off the shelves are those with an Eastern provenance. Indian, Chinese, and Japanese religions are not only exciting because of their newness to a Western student, they are also compatible with the modern scientific world-view in a way that Christianity is not. It is common knowledge that distinguished exponents of the new physics that has developed from the work of Einstein, Bohr, Planck, and Heisenberg are impressed by the similarities between this view of reality and the one found in Eastern religions. Fritjof Capra's much-praised book *The Tao of Physics* sees the cosmic dance as the clue to the nature of the physical world, and the cover of his book is adorned with the well-known image of the dancing Siva. I have often been struck by the fact that, among the Hindus who are leaders in theoretical and practical scientific work, I have never detected any such conflict between science and religion as we have had in Europe.

The reason is clear. The Eastern religions do not understand the world in terms of purpose. The symbol of the dance is an interpretation of movement and change without invoking the idea of purpose. The Bible, on the other hand, is dominated by the idea of divine purpose. This means that one has to say that value judgments are either right or wrong in that they are or are not directed to the end for which all things in fact exist.

This excursion into the recent experience of British schools has led me to an important point. The Indian atomic scientists (most of them trained by Western missionaries) and their counterparts in the rest of Asia are a reminder of the fact that the culture I have called modern Western is at present a world culture and exercises the dominant role everywhere. In almost every country of the world, to modernize is to accept this way of viewing things and this way of doing things. As I have said, the Eastern religions find it easy to be at home in this modern scientific world. And this in turn strengthens those elements in Western Christendom that have tried to find a place for religion within the world-view of post-Enlightenment Europe. Within this world-view it is possible to keep a place for religion as a deeply inward and private experience, whether understood in terms of pure mysticism or in terms of some sort of loving dependence on the ultimate source of being. In this experience people of all religions can find a kinship. It does not challenge the dominant scientific world-view but keeps, so to speak, a private place for religion within the public world of scientifically understood facts. Many writers have celebrated this shared experience and have seen it as the center around which the great world religions could move into unity.

There is something very attractive about this view. It promises peace, not only between the religions but also between faith and science. It avoids a head-on collision between the two because it does not challenge the scientist's account of how things are; rather, it withdraws into an inner world that the scientist cannot reach, or where, even if he does enter, it is possible to show that there are different kinds of language that can be used, different "language games" that can be played. Yet the one whose world-view is shaped by the Bible finds it hard to accept this. It has often been remarked that Protestant theology since Schleiermacher has had a continual tendency to become a kind of anthropology. It has become the study of an aspect of human experience. The Bible, on the other hand, is dominated by the figure of the living God who acts, speaks, calls, and expects an answer. The biblical language is as much about God, about the created cosmos, and about the world of public events as about what can be called "religious experience." All of this can, of course, be translated into the language of religious experience and then set alongside other transcripts of religious experience in other cultures. And yet one cannot help at least asking the question, "Might it not be otherwise?" What if it were simply a fact that the one by whose will and purpose all things exist, from the galactic system to the electrons and neutrons, has acted and spoken in certain specific events and words in order to reveal and effect his purpose and to call us to respond in love and obedience? If this were a fact, we might still sit down coolly to consider it in relation to other facts. But by doing so we would be asserting our right to make the final decision, and we have no means of proving that we have that right. It might be that we do not, that the history of Western man in the past two hundred years has been shaped by an illusion. And it might be that the signs, manifest all around us, of the disintegration of this culture of ours are ultimately attributable to that illusion.

All I am daring to say at this stage is that it might be so. In order to carry the argument further, I now need to do two things. The first is to look at the strange book we call "*the* Book" (the Bible) and ask what it is and how we can understand its authority. The next is to inquire what would be involved in both theory and practice in such a direct challenge to the very foundations of the culture of which we ourselves are a part. What would it mean if, instead of trying to explain the gospel in terms of our modern scientific culture, we tried to explain our culture in terms of the gospel?

3. The Word in the World

I have defined as the purpose of these chapters the exploration of what would be involved in a missionary encounter between the gospel and our culture. I have tried to sketch a profile of one of these two parties, our culture. It is now necessary to focus attention on the other party, the gospel.

If one begins with the example of cross-cultural mission, one sees a group of people called missionaries who already organize their corporate life around a story that is told in a book and is continually reenacted by word and sacramental action in their liturgy. The encounter between the gospel and the strange culture takes place in a whole complex of contacts between the community organized in this way and the people to whom they come. At an early stage they will begin to translate the book into the language of the people and commend it to them as the word of God calling for their response.

For our modern Western society, both the society and the book are already extremely familiar. They are not perceived as addressing any fresh challenge to our accepted world-view. Critical scholarship, using the tools developed in the past two hundred years, has brought the Bible into the brilliant light of the modern scientific world-view. The story it tells is now placed within the general history of the ancient world and evaluated on the basis of the same criteria that the modern historian uses in his work on any other ancient document. Under this light, the Bible can have no privileged status. It is part of the whole corpus of ancient literature. The events it records are to be understood by placing them within the unbroken network of cause and effect that links all history together. The ideas it expresses, whether in myth, saga, or legend, are to be understood by relating them to the similar beliefs of other ancient peoples. And the religious experience to which it bears witness is to be understood as part of the continuous religious experience of the human race as a whole.

And if the sacred book has been thus desacralized and placed firmly within the world of objective facts that the scientist studies and classifies, so also the sacred society, the church, is desacralized. The more recent techniques of the anthropologist and sociologist have in this century been applied to the church in all its manifestations. The sociologist sees the changing structures of ecclesiastical bodies not as the divinely willed order that is affirmed by the theologian, but as examples of the normal operation of cause and effect as it is to be observed in other human societies.

And who can deny that this kind of scientific study has been enormously illuminating with regard to both the Bible and the church. The "light" in the Enlightenment was real light. We are able in some respects to understand the Bible better than we did before, and we are able in some ways to understand what actually goes on in the life of the church better than we did before the Enlightenment. Whatever else may be possible, it is not possible to put ourselves back before that experience. It is not possible to unknow what we have learned. And it is not possible to prevent that knowledge from becoming the possession of all people of all cultures who desire it.

But how, as men and women who do possess this knowledge, how can we speak of a genuine encounter between the gospel and our culture? What are we speaking of when we speak of the gospel? However we define it—as verbal message, as events in history, as faith embodied in *praxis,* as inward religious experience, or whatever—we are talking about something that is, from the point of view of our culture, already accounted for. It is part of our culture. We know where to place it. It is firmly held within the web of facts, events, and experiences that are all, at least in principle, patient of explanation in terms of the invariable operation of cause and effect. It is all capable of being objectified and studied with the appropriate techniques of modern science in its broadest reach. It is all part of the total world of phenomena that is the business of science to understand and so to master. How can it challenge us? We may use one of Isaiah's parables (in a sense opposite to his) and ask: "Shall the axe vaunt itself against him who hews with it?" (Isa. 10:15). The Bible and the church are part of our culture. How shall a part of our culture make claims against our culture? Is there any meaning in speaking of an encounter?

It is well known that the first and perhaps still one of the most massive attempts to affirm the gospel in the context of post-Enlightenment culture was that of Schleiermacher, and it can truly be said that all subsequent theological work in the Protestant West has been done under his shadow. In *The Christian Faith* Schleiermacher defined the nature of theology in terms that place it firmly on one side of the divide between the world of public facts and the world of private values. "Christian doctrines," he writes, "are accounts of the Christian religious affections set forth in speech." They are the transcripts of "the religious self-consciousness." Insofar as Christian theology incorporates statements about the attributes and acts of God or about the constitution of the world, it must be understood that these are not properly part of dogmatics, that they belong respectively to metaphysics and natural science; they "belong to the objective consciousness and its conditions, and are independent of the inner experience and the facts of the higher self-consciousness." "We must declare the description of human states of mind to be the fundamental dogmatic form; while propositions about the second and third forms (i.e., about the attributes and acts of God, or the constitution of the world) are permissible only insofar as they can be developed out of propositions of the first form." That matter becomes very clear in Schleiermacher's brief treatment of the resurrection of Jesus from the dead. He consistently speaks of this as a fact but absolutely denies that it has any bearing on faith in Jesus as Redeemer, which is the heart of the self-consciousness of the Christian believer.[1]

It is clear from statements such as these that Schleiermacher was fencing off an area of inward religious experience that would be protected from the otherwise total dominance of an "objectifying consciousness" (to use his phrase), from a world of hard fact ultimately explicable on the terms provided by Newtonian science. It is also

1. F. Schleiermacher, *The Christian Faith,* para. 15, p. 76; para. 30, p. 126; para. 97, pp. 418ff.

clear why subsequent Protestant theology has always seemed to tremble on the edge of falling into pure anthropology, so that theological statements were thought to have no referent except the religious consciousness itself. And it is clear that Feuerbach was only drawing the obvious conclusion when he said that the very idea of God is a *brockenspecter,* the projection of an image of the human ego onto the cosmos. Such an understanding of theology could perhaps, at least until the arrival of modern psychology, provide a hiding place for religion from the searing light of science, a space within the modern world for the continued cultivation of an archaic form of self-consciousness. But it could not challenge the ideology that ruled the public world.

We are familiar with the kind of liberal theology so characteristic of the later nineteenth and the twentieth centuries in which the boundaries of what is possible to believe were firmly fixed by the axioms of the Enlightenment, in which it was taken for granted that the modern scientific world-view provides the only reliable account of how things really are, and that the Bible has to be understood only in terms of that account. This required a reconstruction of biblical history on the lines of modern historical science. It required the elimination of miracle. It dictated that while the crucifixion of Jesus could be accepted as a fact of real history, his resurrection was a psychological experience of the disciples. Insofar as the biblical scholar recognized religion as an authentic fact of human experience, he could find in the Bible testimony to religion, perhaps to the supreme and definitive experience of the religious spirit. But intellectual integrity required that the Bible must be understood in terms of what it is possible for a modern person to believe.

Many different strategies have been developed in the attempt to retain an authentic place for the Bible in the post-Enlightenment world. One was to continue to assert as a matter of faith that the Bible is a factually accurate account of creation and history and that where the account is contradicted by modern science, modern science is wrong. About this strategy we may say three things: 1)

It is difficult to maintain without a kind of split personality if one is going to live an active life in the modern world. As Langdon Gilkey has remarked, even the most devout fundamentalist in Texas, when prospecting for oil, consults the geologists and not the biblical scholars.[2] 2) Those who hold this position are themselves part of the modern world; consequently, when they say that the Bible is factually accurate, they are working with a whole context of meaning, within a concept of factuality that is foreign to the Bible. Fundamentalism in this form is a post-Enlightenment product. 3) Perhaps the ablest theologian among those who have espoused this position is Benjamin Warfield, and it has been pointed out[3] that in the last analysis Warfield's position rests upon a reference to experience, to the church's perennial experience of the Bible as something that has evoked and continues to evoke awe, reverence, a sense of the holy. In fact, Warfield finds the ultimate authority of Scripture at a point where he is speaking a language that Schleiermacher would have acknowledged as authentic.

Much more common than this has been the strategy that seeks to conserve the religious meaning of the Bible without any attempt to defend its factual accuracy in matters of natural science or history. This recognizes that the biblical writers were people of their own times, ignorant of many things we know, and limited by the intellectual tools available to them. Consequently, their accounts of material phenomena and historical events have to be examined with the critical tools available to us. But this can lead to a situation in which the scholar simply subjects the biblical text to the same kind of critical analysis that he would use in the case of any other text of similar antiquity. The scholar is the active subject; the Bible is passive object. Its material is to be interpreted in terms of the scholar's total understanding of what is the case, of how things have happened and can happen. The scholar works within the accepted view of how things are, which takes

2. Langdon Gilkey, *How the Church Can Minister to the World without Losing Itself,* p. 91.
3. D. Kelsey, *Uses of Scripture in Recent Theology.*

it for granted that all causes are adequate to the effects they produce, and that events are to be understood by relating them to antecedent causes. The scholar examines the text but is not, in any profound sense, examined by it. If he is a believer, he will draw from the text illumination for his own faith. But his faith does not rest on the authority of the text. It is rather that he perceives a congruence between the faith to which the text bears witness and his own.

But the scholar's training in the skills of the modern critical historian warns him against a simple transference from the religious world of the Bible to his own. He is aware that that world was so different from his that he cannot simply reproduce the religious experiences of the biblical writer or the biblical character. Some scholars are so impressed by the gulf that separates the biblical writers from ourselves that they nearly deny any possibility of communication across it, since "we cannot understand the word 'God' in any of the ways in which Old Testament Jews understood the name Yahweh or even in the ways in which New Testament writers understood the word 'Theos.'"[4] Such an extreme skepticism both denies the fundamental unity of human nature and also implicitly absolutizes a certain twentieth-century world-view. But it represents merely the extreme development of a way of treating the Bible that so fixes it like a fossil embodied in ancient strata that it cannot speak to us today except as exemplifying forms of the universal religious experience that can be paralleled in other parts of the human story.

Another way of seeking to relate the Bible to the post-Enlightenment world has been to distill from it concepts or principles that could be applied to modern life. During the period of what was called biblical theology, much was made of distinctively biblical concepts that enable one to deal with reality in distinctive ways. In an earlier period the attempt was made to draw principles for conduct from the Bible. William Temple's influential writings on church and society were a good illustration. Once again, it is not the text of the Bible itself that functions as authority but

---

4. D. Nineham, *The Use and Abuse of the Bible*, p. 237.

the concepts or principles that can be extracted from it. And it is not clear that these derive their authority from the fact that they are extracted from the Bible. Or to put it more exactly, it is not clear what their provenance in the Bible gives them or why it should give them any authority other than the authority that their intrinsic rightness may give them to the reason and conscience of modern men and women.

Another strategy has been to concentrate on the character of the Bible as history—the history of the acts of God. God's revelation of himself, in this view, is not in the text itself but in the events reported and interpreted in the text. The Bible is the record of the acts of God, not a compendium of teaching about God; the story behind the text rather than the text itself is the locus of God's revelation. It is for the modern believer to understand the story of these acts, the salvation history, in contemporary terms. This view thus parts company with the two previous ones in accepting the reality of divine action in history. But it is not always clear whether the series of divine acts that constitute the salvation history is to be understood as forming the central thread of universal history, thus replacing the world history taught in secular academies, or whether it is understood as the clue to the specifically religious experience that is available as a personal option within the public history. Salvation history (*Heilsgeschichte*) is sometimes portrayed as something quite distinct from the ordinary history depicted by secular historians and immune from their critical investigations. In this case it is clear that we are still caught in the familiar dichotomy. *Heilsgeschichte* belongs to the private world; the public world has a different kind of history.

Very notable among contemporary appeals to Scripture is the work of Rudolf Bultmann and the many biblical scholars who have been influenced by him. Here one can say that the relationship between the scholar and the text is emphatically not that of subject and object. Here the text is indeed allowed to address the reader; but it can do so only in the pure immediacy of subject to subject. The encounter has nothing to do with a world of objective facts. Faith is not faith if it seeks security in what are called facts—whether metaphysical or historical. To seek this kind of security is to seek a sort of justification by works and is the antithesis of genuine faith. "Faith," says Bultmann, "must not aspire to an objective basis in dogma or in history on pain of losing its character as faith."[5] Consequently, Bultmann and his followers can cheerfully accept the dissolution of most of the historical material in the gospels in the powerful acids of scientific criticism and yet find in the New Testament that which summons them to faith understood as authentic existence. It is very obvious that we are here firmly within the post-Kantian world, in which fact and value have no intrinsic relationship to each other. Bultmann seems to accept uncritically the so-called scientific account of nature and history that claims to provide secure knowledge of objective facts apart from any call to faith on the part of the knowing subject. By contrast, the authentic existence that is the essence of faith belongs to a world for which neither science nor history in its secular sense can have anything to say. It belongs exclusively to the private world.

If we admit the dichotomy of fact and value, then it would seem that we are indeed bound to admit Bultmann's claim that to rely on so-called objective facts of history or of science is in conflict with the evangelical call to be justified by faith alone. Bultmann and his successors do seek to enable the modern person belonging to a post-Enlightenment culture to hear himself or herself addressed by a call to faith from Scripture. They argue powerfully that, as practiced by them, the work of radical historical criticism of the Bible is implied by the Reformation doctrine of justification by faith alone. But what has to be asked is whether this call of the gospel is addressed only to the individual in the privacy of his own soul or whether it does not also call into question the claim of the modern world that the scientific study of nature and history can provide a sort of knowledge that is secure, is not open to doubt, and does not depend on faith. Can room really be made for faith in the private

5. R. Bultmann, *Faith and Understanding*, p. 41.

world if it is banished from the public world as merely a poor substitute for secure knowledge? And, to turn the same argument the other way around, does not consistency require us even to eliminate the name of Jesus altogether from this account of authentic existence—except for illustrative purposes? If the objective facts of history form no part of the foundation for faith, why do we need to invoke that name? The Christ of faith could, it would seem, function very well on Bultmann's terms without being confused by any sort of association with the so-called Jesus of history. And is "faith" the proper name for something that is merely a psychological condition and has no cognitive element—has no object about which ontological claims can be made?

The dichotomy between a world of so-called objective facts that can be "scientifically" known apart from any faith commitment on the part of the knower and a world of beliefs that are solely the personal responsibility of the believer is precisely what has to be questioned in the light of the gospel. This will be our concern in the next chapter. Here it must be said that if such a dichotomy were to be accepted, Bultmann and his followers would be correct in rejecting any foundation for faith in the so-called facts of history. But it should not be accepted.

All the strategies I have described in such cursory fashion have this in common: they operate within the cultural presuppositions of the modern scientific world-view. That is obvious. But is it not also inevitable? Is it possible to read Scripture in any other way than as the people we are? Can we set aside the axioms and assumptions we share with our contemporaries in all our daily business and conversations, which have shaped the whole of our education, which we accept not deliberately by choice but inevitably and apart from any decision to do so, simply because this is how things in fact are? Is this not how we are bound to see things if we are to sustain our integrity? The Bible is not an extraterritorial entity that has been dropped into our world from another; it is part of our world. Are we not therefore bound to interpret it by means of the only categories of thought we have? How, indeed, can it influence us at all, except as it speaks to us in our language as part of the real world we inhabit?

In asking these rhetorical questions, I am not forgetting all that has been written about the famous hermeneutical circle. No one comes to any text with a completely vacant mind. Everyone comes with a pre-understanding; without this no understanding is possible. But the reader must also, in a sense, place a temporary moratorium on his judgment, allow the text to speak in its own way, and accept the possibility that the pre-understanding will be changed into a new understanding. The path of the true hermeneutic thus runs between two dangers: one is emphasizing the strangeness, the otherness of the text so much that it remains to the end only an object of study that does not call into question the pre-understanding of the reader but leaves his mental world unchanged except for the addition of some new facts; the other danger is failing to recognize the otherness of the text so much that one simply absorbs it into the already existing pre-understanding of the reader. Plainly, these observations are applicable to the reading and understanding of Scripture. We come to it, inevitably, with the pre-understanding into which we have been nurtured by our culture. It cannot be otherwise. But we must ask whether the model of the hermeneutic circle is adequate to describe what is involved in the encounter between Scripture and our culture.

In asking this question, I have in mind the many passages of Scripture that emphasize the incomprehensibility of its message by the wisdom of this world, the radical discontinuity between all human wisdom, even the most profound, and the revelation with which Scripture is concerned. I have in mind the terrible words of Jesus in which he quotes from the sixth chapter of Isaiah to warn that, except to those to whom it is given, his teaching will create not understanding but blindness and hardness of heart (Mark 4:11-12). I have in mind the words of Paul to the effect that the preaching of the gospel, except to those who are called to be its witnesses, is either intolerable or incomprehensible (1 Cor. 1:25-26). Clearly, this kind of language implies a relationship between pre-understanding and understanding that is (to put it no more strongly) not adequately represented by the model of the hermeneutical circle. It implies a profound discontinuity—not just a circle but a chasm.

Of course, to speak of total discontinuity would be absurd. If the discontinuity were total, there could be no awareness of it on either side. There is an analogy in the field of natural science that is, I think, helpful. It is an analogy, no more. Since the publication of Thomas Kuhn's *The Structure of Scientific Revolutions,* we have been familiar with the idea of what he calls "paradigm shifts" in scientific work. I am aware that his thesis has been criticized, and I would certainly not want to imply that scientific theories are merely convenient ways of organizing data rather than ways of seeing what really is the case. Whatever valid criticisms may be made of Kuhn, however, he does demonstrate that shifts such as that from the physics of Newton to that of Einstein do not arise from any step-by-step reasoning from within the presuppositions of the earlier view but from a new vision that calls for a kind of conversion. My point here is simply this: while there is radical discontinuity in the sense that the new theory is not reached by any process of logical reasoning from the old, there is also a continuity in the sense that the old can be rationally understood from the point of view of the new. In Einstein's physics, Newtonian laws are still valid for large bodies in slow motion. Newtonian physics is still valid for mechanics. Thus, to recognize a radical discontinuity between the old and the new is not to surrender to irrationality. Seen from one side there is only a chasm; seen from the other there is a bridge.

By analogy, one could suggest that the radical conversion the Bible speaks about does indeed imply a discontinuity that cannot be acknowledged in the model of the hermeneutical circle. And yet it does not imply a surrender to irrationality, since the new understanding of the converted person might make it possible (no more than this is claimed at the moment) to find a place for the truth that was embodied in the former vision and yet at the same time offer a wider and more inclusive rationality than the older one could. Saul the Pharisee can only see Jesus of Nazareth as a saboteur of the law. Paul the Christian can see the law as the *paidagogos* that brought him to Christ; and he can see Christ as the fulfillment of the law.

I shall return in a moment to the importance of the hermeneutical circle; but here I am only concerned to affirm that the model of the hermeneutical circle is not adequate to account for what is involved in the relationship between the gospel and this or any other culture. I suppose that the boldest and most brilliant essay in the communication of the gospel to a particular culture in all Christian history is the gospel according to John. Here the language and the thought-forms of that Hellenistic world are so employed that Gnostics in all ages have thought that the book was written especially for them. And yet nowhere in Scripture is the absolute contradiction between the word of God and human culture stated with more terrible clarity. The first twelve chapters trace with relentless and cumulative power the total inability of even the best and most godly to grasp what is being offered; and they end with the absolute rejection of Jesus as a blasphemous sinner and with the judgment of the disciples of Moses as children of the devil. And then, from Chapter 13 to 17 we find ourselves in an entirely different world, a world in which Jesus himself is the radiating center of light and love, and all circumstances and future history are illuminated and made meaningful by that light and love. The relationship between these two situations can in no way be described in terms of the hermeneutical circle. On the one side, Jesus is the one who subverts true religion and contradicts ordinary rationality; on the other, he is the center and the source of all truth. The boundary between the two worlds is defined in terms of death and rebirth. And those on this side of the boundary are not those who have been able to make a sort of gigantic hermeneutical leap but those who have been chosen and called—not of their own will—to be the witnesses of Jesus to the world.

When the matter is stated in this way, we who are part of contemporary Western culture are inclined simply to reject such a scenario as irrational. Indeed, we are bound to do so from within this culture. The Christian claim is that, though that other way of understanding the world can in no way be reached by any logical step from the axioms of this one, nevertheless that other way does offer a wider rationality that embraces and does not contradict the rationality of this. We have to test that claim in a later chapter. Here and now we have to look at what this claim involves for our understanding of the hermeneutical circle.

Contemporary exponents of the sociology of knowledge have made us familiar with the fact that our sense of what is real is, to a large extent, a function of the society in which we live. It is almost impossible for an individual to deny steadily the reality of things that society regards as real, or to affirm the reality of things that society regards as illusions. The plausibility structures that largely control our perception of what is the case are socially produced. This is true whether we are talking about tightly knit religious societies such as Islam or about our modern pluralistic societies that treat religious confraternities simply as manifestations of options taken by groups of individuals for the private sector of their lives. The modern scientific world-view functions as a plausibility structure in the same way as does Islam or Catholicism. This is not, of course, to say anything about the truth of the views embodied in these structures, but only about the way they function in limiting the freedom of the individual in deciding questions about truth.

The awe-inspiring achievements of modern science in the past 250 years have been based, we recall, on the methodological elimination of the idea of purpose from the study of phenomena. The model of explanation accepted by modern science is one that exhibits the cause-and-effect relationship between phenomena. Even at points where the model seems—at least for the time being—to falter, as in the case of quantum physics, no scientist will suggest that the particles in question act from conscious purpose or as the result of supernatural intervention. The success of this method has been so overwhelming that a failure to find an explanation within its terms is treated simply as a temporary setback and not as grounds for doubting the method. And it is surely inevitable that the Bible should be subjected to the same methods of study, methods assuming that its contents can be explained without reference to a divine purpose controlling events. To one whose mental world is wholly shaped by the modern scientific world-view, the statement "God acted at this and this point in the explanation of the story" simply does not "explain." It does not belong to the world of real causes. He will be bound to attempt some kind of "translation." He recognizes that the biblical writers shared with their contemporaries a world-view in which divine intervention was accepted as an explanation. He, however, lives in a different world. If the text is not to be treated as merely an archaeological specimen, an example of an interesting but now extinct form of human consciousness, it at least has to be translated in order to have any contemporary meaning within the world we inhabit. We are familiar with the various ways in which the translation is done.

But there is another possibility, one for which reasons can be given even within the terms of modern thought. The Bible is not a collection of documents recently dug up in the sands of Egypt. It is quite "unscientific" to treat it as if it were. The Bible comes into our hands as the book of a community, and neither the book nor the community are properly understood except in their reciprocal relationship with each other. Quite clearly, the community as it now exists is being continuously shaped by the attention it gives to the Bible. Equally clearly, the community's reading of the Bible is shaped by a tradition that has been developed through the experience of previous generations of believers in seeking to understand and put into practice the meaning of the book. The "pre-understanding" with which the contemporary community comes to its reading of the Bible is shaped by the ways in which previous generations of Christians have come to understand it in the course of their discipleship. Every Christian reader comes to the Bible with the spectacles provided by the tradition that is alive in the community to which he or she belongs, and that tradition is being constantly modified as each new generation of believers endeavors to be faithful in understanding and living out Scripture. This is the hermeneutical circle operating *within the believing community.*

And precisely this gives us the clue to understanding the nature of the Bible itself. For it has become very clear that Scripture as we have it is the result of the operation of this same hermeneutical circle from the very beginning. Modern scholarship, using the tools of historical and literary criticism developed since the Enlightenment, has enabled us to see that the present text of Scripture as we have it is the result of just such a continuous reshaping of tradition in the light of new experience. Generation after generation, the story has been retold so as to bring out its relevance to the contemporary situation. Today, therefore, as the result of critical scholarship, we are able to read the text in a way that former generations could not. It is not a uniform corpus of "dead" facts and sayings from the past. It is part of a living process in which we share with all who have gone before us in the school of discipleship, and with all who are our contemporaries in the same school. We can ask such questions as: What actually happened? How did this writer understand it? How did the other writer reinterpret the tradition he received? From what source did this word, this idea, this image come? What did the earlier writer mean, and how does this differ from what the later writer understood? But we ask these questions from within our commitment to faith and discipleship, which has been shaped by the tradition in which we share as members of the community that acknowledges the book as authoritative. We are also continually retelling the story in its relevance to ever-new situations.

The asking and answering of all these questions can greatly enhance our understanding, provided it is within the context of the same ultimate faith that governs the life of the whole community, and of our contemporary struggle to understand and be faithful in our own time. The relationship between these two kinds of concern may perhaps be illustrated by the familiar example of the pianist. A great pianist must, at the proper time, concentrate all possible attention on the precise detail of finger movements. But if she attends to these alone while playing a sonata at a concert, the result will be disaster. While she plays, all her mind and soul must be wrapped up in the glory of the music, completely forgetting the finger work. And yet she will lose the glory of the music if she has not done the finger work. It is, of course, possible to study the movements of the pianist's fingers simply as an example of the operation of mechanical, chemical, and electrical principles. A completely self-consistent account of these movements could be given by using these principles. It could be done by a person who is tone-deaf and for whom a Mozart sonata is merely a jumble of noises. But any explanation insisting that this was the only "scientific" way of understanding what is going on would be an odd kind of "science" indeed. It would surely be equally unscientific not to recognize that the reason our universities, even purely secular ones, continue to devote huge resources to the historical-critical study of Scripture—resources far out of proportion to those devoted to other ancient documents—is that these Scriptures have functioned and continue to function in this reciprocal relationship with living communities of faith. It is this relationship that is the clue to their meaning. And it is surely a very unscientific kind of science that supposes that the clue to their meaning is to be found by treating them as fragments from a past we can hardly reconstruct except by a great deal of guesswork. Rather, we must affirm, in the words of Stuhlmacher, that "the biblical texts can be fully interpreted only from a dialogical situation defined by the venture of Christian existence as it is lived in the Church."[6] To recognize this is to recognize also the validity of the "sociology of knowledge" ap-

6. P. Stuhlmacher, *Historical Criticism and Theological Interpretation of Scripture,* p. 89.

proach used by Peter Berger in his apologetic. The Bible functions as authority only within a community that is committed to faith and obedience and is embodying that commitment in an active discipleship that embraces the whole of life, public and private. This is the plausibility structure within which the faith is nourished. Although it may be very shocking to a certain kind of post-Enlightenment Protestant conscience, it is not the Bible by itself but the church confessing the mystery of faith that is spoken of as the pillar and bulwark of the truth (1 Tim. 3:15-16).

I have spoken of the hermeneutical circle that operates within the community of faith. Scripture and tradition, tradition and Scripture are in a constantly developing reciprocal relationship, and the development is not a merely cerebral process but is part of a total life of worship, of obedience, of side-taking discipleship in the ever-changing circumstances of new generations and new cultures. But I have asserted that it is not possible to use the model of the hermeneutical circle to account for what happens at the boundary between this community of faith and the world that lives without this faith. I have suggested that at this boundary one has to use other models—such as are suggested by the biblical image of death and birth. It is obvious that our modern Western world constitutes a plausibility structure within which the biblical account of things is simply unacceptable. It does not correspond to reality as we know it. It is therefore natural that the demand should be made that the language of the Bible should be translated into the terms of our culture so that it may correspond to reality as we know it. We have looked briefly at some of the proposals for doing this. In the next chapter I shall try to show that it is not irrational to propose that a wholly different plausibility structure is possible, that a paradigm shift is possible which—while not logically necessary—does not deny the reason that operates within the contemporary plausibility structure. At the end of this chapter, I wish merely to say something further about the relationship between Scripture and tradition and the sense in which, within the reciprocity of this relation, it is Scripture that always has the primacy.

Earlier in this chapter I have briefly referred to some of the ways in which the post-Enlightenment world has sought to identify the locus of divine revelation and therefore of authority in Scripture. There is the fundamentalist attempt to assert that Scripture is a body of factually inerrant statements about nature and history that must be maintained even when contradicted by modern science. There is the view that Scripture bears witness to authentic personal experience (an experience in whatever terms this may be understood) that is continuous with the total religious experience of the human race. There is the view that Scripture embodies concepts and principles that can be distilled from its material and can stand in their own right as having intrinsic authority. And finally, there is the view that locates the divine revelation in the history behind the story, in the events the biblical writer sought—no doubt with limited understanding—to record and interpret. This "salvation history" is to be distinguished from the history secular historians seek to reconstruct and is therefore immune from their critical assault.

In distinction from all this (and in line with what I have learned from Hans Frei, George Lindbeck, and others), I would want to speak of the Bible as that body of literature which—primarily but not only in narrative form—renders accessible to us the character and actions and purposes of God. In Frei's language, the biblical literature is "realistic narrative," which he defines as that

> in which character or individual persons in their internal depth or subjectivity, as well as in their capacity as doers and sufferers of actions and events, are firmly and significantly set in the context of the external environment, natural but more particularly social . . . that kind in which subject and social setting belong together, and character and external circumstances fitly render each other. . . .Neither is a shadow of something more real or more significant.[7]

In this view, the Bible, taken as a whole, fitly renders God, who is not merely the correlate or referent of universal natural religious experience but is the author and sustainer of all things. But this fitness can only be understood as

---

7. H. Frei, *The Eclipse of Biblical Narrative*, pp. 13-14.

we ourselves are engaged in the same struggle that we see in Scripture, the struggle to understand and deal with the events of our time in the faith that the God revealed in Scripture is in fact the agent whose purpose created and sustained all that is, and will bring it to its proper end. To use the current jargon, the understanding in question simply does not exist apart from *praxis*. And *praxis* means involvement in the public world as much as in the private, since the God who is "rendered" in the Bible is the God of nature and of history as he is of the human soul. The way in which we must read Scripture today is controlled by the fact that we are, from moment to moment in the complex events of our time, dealing with and being dealt with by the same living God who meets us in Scripture, seeking his will, offering our obedience, accepting the share he allots to us of suffering, and looking for the final victory of his cause.

When we speak in these terms, it is clear that we are not talking about a sphere of private religious experience distinct from our experience of life—secular life in this world. To discern God's purpose and to be obedient to it among all the ambiguities and perplexities of life is always a struggle. We may often be wrong both in our understanding of what God is doing and in our attempted obedience, just as it is made clear in Scripture that the people whose stories it tells were often wrong, or only partially right, in their discernment of God's purpose.[8] At best, we can hope to choose the relatively better and to reject the relatively worse. We can never claim that either our understanding or our action is absolutely right. We have no way of proving that we are right. That kind of proof belongs only to the end. As part of the community that shares in the struggle, we open ourselves continually to Scripture, always in company with our fellow disciples of this and former ages and in the context of the struggle for obedience; and we constantly find in it fresh insights into the character and purpose of the one who is "rendered" for us in its pages. We read these pages, naturally, as part of our real history, secular history, the history of which we

---

8. See G. B. Caird, *The Language and Imagery of the Bible*, p. 60.

are a part. What other history is there? There are not different histories, but there are different ways of understanding history. We recognize this because another way of understanding history is being applied to contemporary events around us all the time. It is possible, and in our culture normal, to exclude the name of God altogether from our account of public affairs, and to construe history as a continuum of cause and effect, an arena where "historical forces" are at work and events take place in accordance with regularities that can be scientifically established, or at least an arena in which the only purposes at work are those of individual human beings.

But it is idle to suppose that any kind of peaceful coexistence is possible between these two ways of understanding history. It is clearly an illusion to imagine that there are two kinds of history—sacred and profane, salvation history and secular history. We who are at the moment making and suffering history know that there is only one history, but we know that it can be understood theistically or atheistically. It is true that a methodological atheism may be required in the course of historical study, just as a scientist may eliminate any concern with the music while he studies the movement of the pianist's fingers. But those who belong to the community that is controlled by the rendering of God in Scripture will surely be precluded from a dichotomizing of their lives into a private sphere where God is acknowledged and a public sphere in which events are finally interpreted without reference to God. The long-running debate about the relationship between the Jesus of history and the Christ of faith is simply one manifestation of the illusion that has haunted our culture ever since the Enlightenment. There is only one Jesus, and there is only one history. The question is whether the faith that finds its focus in Jesus is the faith with which we seek to understand the whole of history, or whether we limit this faith to a private world of religion and hand over the public history of the world to other principles of explanation.

The argument hitherto leads to this preliminary conclusion. In the missionary encounter between the gospel and our culture, the first party will be represented by a community for which the Bible is the determinant clue to the character and activity of the one whose purpose is the final meaning of history. The boundary between this community and the society for which the Bible is not determinative is marked by the paradigm shift that is traditionally called conversion. However this conversion may occur— and it can occur in many different ways—those who belong to this community inhabit a different plausibility structure from that of their contemporaries. Things that are myths or illusions for others are real for them. God's power active in world history is not a mythical way of speaking for them, but an account of reality. But it is so only in the context of an active engagement with current events that corresponds to and continually renews this experience.

The difference between the two plausibility structures is seen most sharply at the point where we have to come to terms with the Christian tradition about the resurrection of Jesus. The community of faith makes the confession that God raised Jesus from the dead and that the tomb was empty thereafter. Within the plausibility structure of the "modern world," this will become something like the following: "The disciples had a series of experiences that led them to the belief that, in some sense, Jesus was still alive and therefore to interpret the Cross as victory and not defeat." This experience can be accepted as a "fact." People do have such psychological experiences. If this is what is meant by the "Easter event," then it qualifies for admission to the world of "fact." The former statement (i.e., that the tomb was empty) can be accepted as a fact only if the whole plausibility structure of contemporary Western culture is called into question. To accept it as a fact means that history has a meaning that cannot be found from any study of the regularities and recurrences of the past. It means that the whole existing order of nature and history is confronted by a new reality that gives it a new meaning. It means a radical contradiction of this world as it is. But the affirmation that this is so can be made only by a community that is itself engaged in that contradiction, is actually pitting its life against "the ruler of this world," and—in fellowship with Jesus—is bearing the cost in its own life. All understanding of past events is part of one's understanding of the present and the future. All "facts" of history are remembered and recorded because they have been at some time significant for those engaged in the contemporary struggle of living. The way we understand the past is a function of our whole way of meeting the present and the future. The community of faith celebrates the resurrection of Jesus as the ground of assurance that the present and the future are not under the control of blind forces but are open to unlimited possibilities of new life. This is because the living God who was present in the crucified Jesus is now and always the sovereign Lord of history and therefore makes possible a continuing struggle against all that ignores or negates his purpose.

From the point of view of our contemporary culture, the claim that God raised Jesus from the dead is irrational. It cannot be incorporated into the existing plausibility structure. The widespread phenomenon of "religion," with Christianity regarded as one of its many varieties, can indeed be accommodated without difficulty in our culture. But this claim cannot. It must be regarded as the esoteric belief of a community that is living in a world of make-believe rather than the world of facts. There is no way by which the truth of the claim can be demonstrated within the plausibility structure that shapes the modern mind. It is, of course, equally true that the contemporary dominance of this plausibility structure is no proof of its congruence with reality. But three positive things can be said very briefly by way of a conclusion to this chapter. First, from within the plausibility structure that is shaped by the Bible, it is perfectly possible to acknowledge and cherish the insights of our culture. There is an asymmetry in this relationship, as between the paradigms of science, but not a total discontinuity. From one side the other looks quite irrational, but from the other side there is a rationality that embraces both. This will be the theme of our next chapter.

Second, therefore, the conflict between the two views will not be settled on the basis of logical argument. The view will prevail that is seen to offer—both in theory and in practice—the widest rationality, the greatest capacity to give meaning to the whole of experience. This is as much a matter of faithful endeavor and costly obedience as of clarity and coherence of argument. It is at the heart of the biblical vision of the human situation that the believer is a witness who gives his testimony in a trial where it is contested. The verdict as to what stands and what falls will only be given at the end. To suppose that some kind of rationally conclusive "proof" of one position or the other might be available now is to misunderstand the human situation.

And finally, it follows that the missionary encounter of the gospel with the modern world will, like every true missionary encounter, call for radical conversion. This will be not only a conversion of the will and of the feelings but a conversion of the mind—a "paradigm shift" that leads to a new vision of how things are and, not at once but gradually, to the development of a new plausibility structure in which the most real of all realities is the living God whose character is "rendered" for us in the pages of Scripture.

4. What can we know?
The Dialogue with Science

The most obvious fact that distinguishes our culture from all that have preceded it is that it is—in its public philosophy—atheist. The famous reply of Laplace to the complaint that he had omitted God from his system—"I had no need of that hypothesis"—might stand as a motto for our culture as a whole.

The vision of reality that comes to expression in Laplace's system still dominates, if I am not mistaken, popular thinking today in spite of all the changes in science itself that have taken place since his time. It assumes that the real world is that which can be "scientifically" explained by laws of cause and effect that can be expressed in mathematical terms. Consequently, to quote Laplace, "An intelligence which knew at one moment of time all the forces by which nature is animated and the respective positions of the entities which compose it . . . would embrace in the same formula the movements of the largest bodies in the universe and those of the lightest atoms; nothing would be uncertain for it, and the future, like the past, would be present to its eyes."[1] As Polanyi has pointed out, the person who had this knowledge would know precisely nothing, since the knowledge of the atomic particles of which a thing is composed is not knowledge of the thing. The deceptive power of the formula is that it suppresses what Polanyi calls the tacit dimension of knowledge without which knowing is an impossible undertaking. We are interested in atoms and molecules only because of the part they play in the shaping of a world we know as human beings and before we know anything about physics.

Nevertheless, this Laplacean vision of reality still dominates popular thinking. It sustains "a universal tendency to enhance the observational accuracy and systematic precision of science at the expense of its bearing on the subject matter."[2] It leads to the delusion that when we have discovered the smallest units of which a thing is composed and the forces by which they are moved, we have

---

1. Laplace, *Traité de Probabilité*, 7:vi-vii; quoted in M. Polanyi, *Personal Knowledge*, p. 140.
2. M. Polanyi, *Personal Knowledge*, p. 141.

understood the thing. And this delusion is enormously reinforced by the fact that in societies shaped by our culture the processes of manufacture, exchange, and government are conducted on these principles. A mechanical view of the nature of ultimate reality is made more credible by the fact that we live in a mechanically organized world.

We are familiar with the story of the long rearguard action fought by theologians against the relentless advance of this way of understanding the world. At point after point, attempts have been made to identify the places where the mechanical explanation breaks down and some kind of divine intervention has to be posited as the only explanation. But, as we well know, time after time the gap has been closed and the "God of the gaps" has had to retreat to another temporary refuge. Today the futility of this strategy is generally recognized, in spite of occasional efforts to find a place for divine intervention in the Heisenberg principle of indeterminacy. Theologians and believing scientists have in recent times sought rather a *modus vivendi* between science and religion by representing them as two different ways of seeing the same reality. The insights of gestalt psychology have been utilized to show that as the same objects can be seen in different ways, so the same phenomena can be understood in different but complementary ways so that there need be no quarrel between the two. The same person can be a scientist and a believer, and he can look at the same things in two different ways, depending on whether he is in his laboratory or in church.

It is difficult to remain content with this kind of peaceful coexistence. It is, of course, true that we sometimes see (to use the famous illustration) a picture of two human profiles as if it were a picture of a vase. It is true—in the more famous Indian parable—that one can see a piece of rope as if it were a snake. But no sane person is content to leave matters there. Unless we are to live in a world of make-believe, we will not be content until we have decided which it is—a rope or a snake. Having discovered what it is, we shall then be able to understand the different ways of seeing it—as a snake or as a rope. But we shall not be content until we have reached that point.

To be specific, the currently popular way of coping with the science-religion debate by regarding it as an example of two ways of "seeing as" is, I fear, only a particular manifestation of that dichotomy between the public world of facts and the private world of values about which I have spoken. Of course, if religion is construed in essentially mystical terms—that is, in terms for which the idea of purpose is not central—then there is no clash. The modern scientific world-view coexists peacefully and naturally with that kind of religion. But if we are talking as the Bible talks about God, who is Creator and Governor of all things, who acts in specific ways, and whose purpose is the criterion for everything human, whether in the public or the private sectors, then there is an inevitable conflict. Is it or is it not the case that every human being exists for the joy of eternal fellowship with God and must face the possibility of missing that mark, forfeiting that prize? If it is the case, it ought to be part of the core curriculum in every school. It will not do to say that the determination of character by the structure of the DNA molecule is a fact that any child must learn to understand, but that the determination of all proper human purposes by the glory of God is an opinion that anyone is free to accept or reject. The question of which is the real world simply cannot be permanently evaded. There can be no genuinely missionary encounter of the gospel with our culture unless we face these questions. For there can be no question that for the ordinary educated person in our society, the real world is not the world of the Bible but a world that can be explained, and is being more and more fully explained, without reference to the hypothesis of God.

In spite of all the vast changes in physics in the present century, the vision of the real world in the mind of ordinary inhabitants of our culture is the one derived from Newtonian science. Its essential features are something like the following: There is an infinite world of space that is at rest; it has existed and will exist without beginning or end. In this space there are moving bodies that continually interact at a distance in ways governed by the laws of inertia and gravity. All things that exist consist of such bodies, which are exceedingly small but are nevertheless real and finite things—be they molecules, atoms, electrons, or whatever. This is the real world. Clearly, it has many of the qualities traditionally ascribed to God—infinity, eternity, and absolute rest. In any case, it is the real world. It alone is what we have reliable knowledge of, what we have to do with, what we have to take account of.

We are familiar with the fact that this picture of reality has been drastically changed by a whole series of developments in the past hundred years, including Clark Maxwell's magnetic field theory, Einstein's special and general relativity, quantum physics, and the recent discoveries about the fundamental structure of matter. The new physics is so different from the old that those whose minds have been shaped by the old are almost unable to grasp the new except through long and thorough training. A nonscientist can only tread here with great caution. But some things even a scientifically illiterate theologian can grasp. The universe as modern physics understands it is neither infinite nor eternal. It has a calculable age and, according to the Second Law of Thermodynamics, is moving inexorably toward total entropy, in which nothing that could be called matter will exist. Space and time are no longer two different forms of infinity, but space-time is a single finite entity—liable to "warping," having a beginning at a calculable time-distance from the present, and having also a limit at which it ceases to exist. At this limit, the so-called singularity, space-time no longer exists, and the laws of physics no longer operate. Moreover, there is no "point of absolute rest" from which the universe could be surveyed. All points are relative to all others, and there is only one absolute, namely, the speed of light. Furthermore, the work done on the fundamental structure of matter has led into a world where entities that can hardly be called "things" in any ordinary sense operate according to principles that cannot be described in mechanical terms. There is no way in which the most fundamental elements in the structure of the atom as modern physics understands it can be visualized. Leptons and quarks, muons and photons are not pieces of matter in any imaginable sense. Nor is it possible to form any visual image of anti-matter. "Matter is an affair of changing relationships between non-material entities."[3] Neither the organic images of ancient Greek science nor the mechanical models of Newtonian science have any further validity. The only language that can be used is that of mathematics in a more and more abstruse form. And not even mathematics can provide us with an absolutely secure mental framework any longer, for—according to the famous Gödelian theorems that have never been disproved—within any rigidly logical mathematical system there are propositions (or questions) that cannot be proved or disproved on the basis of the axioms within that system, and consequently it is uncertain that the basic axioms of arithmetic will not give rise to contradictions. We are a very long way from the Newtonian world. Yet it is the Newtonian view that still largely shapes our culture, both its way of thinking and its way of organizing its public life.

At this point it is helpful to draw attention to two elements in the history of thought since the rise of modern science. The first is this. Both science and theology have been reluctant in recent decades to enter into the discussion of cosmology. Theology has been reluctant because it has shared in the general withdrawal of religion to the private sector. It was willing to discuss time and history because personal being is so intimately involved in time; but it was not interested in space. As we have seen, even its discussion of history was drawn toward a special *Heilsgeschichte,* separate from a so-called scientific history, which deals with events in space. Theology has tended to become anthropology, or rather psychology. On the other hand, science has until recently avoided cosmology for fear of becoming involved in metaphysical questions for which traditional physics has no answers. But today the

3. W. H. Thorpe, *Purpose in a World of Chance: A Biologist's View,* p. 111.

advance of astrophysics has carried it to the limits of the universe and forced it to face cosmological questions that are ultimately metaphysical. Physics thus challenges theology in a new way to come out of its private enclave and say what it has to say about the world, about the single finite entity the physicists call space-time, within which it is impossible to isolate a "spiritual" world of time from a "material" world of space.

The other point is this. Studies in the origin and development of modern science have led historians to ask why the brilliant intellectual powers of the ancient Chinese, Indians, Egyptians, and Greeks, in spite of their achievements both in observation and in pure speculation, never brought forth the dynamic, self-developing science of the modern era.[4] It has been very plausibly argued that the decisive factor is to be found in the biblical vision of the world as both rational and contingent. For to put it briefly, if the world is not rational, science is not possible; if the world is not contingent, science is not necessary. Let me put the point more fully: On the one hand, the enterprise of science would be impossible if there were no principle of rationality in the universe. If every instrument reading in a laboratory were simply an isolated happening that could not be connected in an intelligible way with other readings, the whole enterprise would be futile. But, in fact, a scientist faced with an apparent irrationality does not accept it as final, nor does he take refuge in the idea of arbitrary divine intervention. He goes on struggling to find some rational way in which the facts can be related to each other, some formula or mathematical equation that will tie them logically together. This struggle is a deeply passionate one, sustained by the faith that there must be a solution even though no one can yet say what it is. Without that passionate faith in the ultimate rationality of the world, science would falter, stagnate, and die—as has happened before. Thus science is sustained in its search for an understanding of what it sees by faith in

---

4. E. G. Stanley Jaki, *Science and Creation* (1974); *The Road of Science and the Ways to God* (1978).

what is unseen. The formula *credo ut intelligam* is fundamental to science.

But—and this is the other equally important fact—faith in the rationality of the universe would not sustain science without the concurrent belief that the universe is not necessary being but contingent being. Indian metaphysics has been totally committed to the rationality of the universe but has understood it as necessary being—part of the eternal cycle of evolution and involution. The universe is the emanation of Brahma, not the creation of a personal God. Its ultimate secrets are therefore to be discovered within the recesses of the human soul, where it makes direct contact with the cosmic soul. The discovery does not depend on meticulous observation of empirical phenomena and painstaking experiments to test theory against the findings of observation. Science in the sense in which it has developed in our culture is not impossible, but it is unnecessary. Consequently, in the great cultures of China, India, and Egypt, in spite of the brilliant intellectual powers they have manifested, science in the modern sense did not develop. And even Greece, which came closer than any other ancient culture to developing a viable science, failed to do so and relapsed into the ancient idea of a cyclical universe—the most pervasive form of belief in a world that is rational but not contingent. A developed science can, as we have seen in modern examples, peacefully exist within this kind of monistic worldview where the universe is seen as the necessary form of an immanent rationality; but such a world-view cannot, it seems, give birth to a spontaneously developing science. It can coexist with it but it cannot create it. The necessary precondition for the birth of science as we know it is, it would seem, the diffusion through society of the belief that the universe is both rational and contingent. Such a belief is the presupposition of modern science and cannot by any conceivable argument be a product of science. One has to ask: Upon what is this belief founded?

I hope that the relevance of this twofold excursion into the history of science will become clear as we proceed. The first point to be made is this: It is clear that what one may call the "methodological atheism" of modern science has been part of the clue to its dazzling success. It was and is part of the recognition of contingency in the nature of things. As long as scientific thought was controlled by the idea of perfect numbers and perfect circles, or by the concept of the purposeful organism (and both of these were legacies of Greek science)—in other words, as long as it was controlled by the idea of a completely immanent rationality—the breakthrough to modern science could not occur. It could only do so by virtue of a firm determination to study the phenomena and, so to speak, to allow them to speak for themselves. But by the same token, it is easy to see that a purely mechanistic vision of the ultimate nature of things is equally certain to become a fetter on the development of genuine science. And we have seen how the advances in physics during the present century have rendered implausible this mechanistic vision, and indeed any form of purely immanent rationality. Contemporary physics recognizes a finite and therefore contingent universe. It acknowledges limits beyond which its own axioms do not operate, and this again is a recognition of contingency. And in the Gödelian theorems, it recognizes that mathematics itself does not consist of absolute and eternally necessary truths but has in it an element of contingency.

Moreover, it has become clear that even infinitesimally small differences in the original explosion that cosmologists see as the starting point of our universe would have resulted in a world in which conscious life would not occur. In other words, ours is only one among billions of possible worlds, all of them equally rational. This has given rise to the so-called anthropic principle, which in its weak form states that our location in the universe is necessarily privileged to the extent of being compatible with our existence as observers, and in its strong form states that the universe must be such as to admit the creation of observers within it. In both formulations this looks like an attempt to impose an immanent and necessary rationality on facts that suggest radical contingency. As far as physics can tell us, there could have been billions of other universes; there is, for us at least, only this one. We possess no powers of reasoning that can show that it had to be this one, unless we start by assuming that our consciousness is the measure of all things.

These new developments in physics and cosmology open the way for a real dialogue between believers and scientists such as was impossible when the mechanistic model dominated physics. Our missionary task, however, is rendered more difficult by the fact that other branches of science are still so largely controlled by mechanistic models. Thus one can observe the peculiar fact that precisely during the period when mechanical models in physics were breaking down, biologists were abandoning earlier vitalist theories and trying to describe the phenomena of plant and animal life in mechanistic terms—and this in spite of the extensive demonstrations of the capacity of even very lowly animals to recognize and solve problems, in other words, to engage in purposeful activity. F. H. C. Crick, whose discovery of the DNA molecule has had such a profound effect on popular thinking about the nature of life, is quoted as saying that "the ultimate aim of the modern movement in biology is in fact to explain all biology in terms of physics and chemistry,"[5] and there is no doubt that this reductionist way of thinking is very widespread. Yet its absurdity is obvious, for not even a machine can be explained by the chemical and physical analyses of its component wheels and shafts and pulleys. It is possible to show how the functioning of each part contributes to the operation of the whole, but it would be absurd to say that we have "explained" the machine as a whole if we have no idea of the purpose for which it was designed and built. It is explained by understanding its purpose. And biologists have shown that the discovery of the physical basis of the genetic code in the DNA molecule, so far from explaining the origin of life, made it more mysterious. Even if we assume that the genetic code is the chance product of natural selection, it is without biological function until it is translated, and the machinery for

5. From *Of Molecules and Men* (1966), quoted in A. R. Peacocke, *Creation and the World of Science,* p. 118.

this translation depends on components that are themselves the products of the translation. The possibility of this occurring by chance is so small as to amount to zero probability, so that even Crick has seriously suggested that life may have been transmitted to this planet from some other part of space.[6] To say these things, of course, in no way questions the enormous importance of these discoveries about the physical and chemical conditions for the existence of life. It merely denies that the knowledge of these conditions constitutes an explanation.

In a similar way, the enormous advances in our knowledge of the structure and functioning of the brain have been used to disseminate the idea that the objects we call our minds have no real existence, and that what we experience as our own mental life is to be fully "explained" as the functioning of approximately ten billion electrical circuits in the cerebral cortex, and therefore that it is in principle possible to create an electronic computer that will be equivalent to a human being in its mental operation. Again, to attack this is not to call into question the great fruitfulness of our increased knowledge of the physical condition of mental life. It is to point out that to regard knowledge of these conditions as an explanation leads to absurdity. One way of stating the absurdity is as follows: however we may explain our mental states, we know that we have them. I think that I exist. If this idea is only a series of electrical pulses in my brain, the capacity of the brain to produce these pulses must be the result of evolution by natural selection. But since the idea that I can by my will affect the operation of these pulses is an illusion, the existence of this idea can have no effect upon what happens in the world of physical and chemical change. Therefore, it can have no bearing on natural selection. Therefore, the existence of this illusion is an unexplained mystery since it cannot have arisen from natural selection. The "explanation" fails to explain.

Everyone is aware of the difference between a movement of his hand that is consciously performed for a purpose and a movement brought about by applying an

6. Quoted in Thorpe, *Purpose in a World of Chance*, p. 26.

electrical current from a battery to the appropriate nerve. It may seem a waste of time to point out that they are not the same. We know perfectly well the difference between a responsible action and an involuntary jerk. And yet the power of the mechanistic image is so great that it permeates the mind of our culture with the idea that "explanation" must be in its terms, and that to explain behavior in terms of the responsible action of a person who is capable of understanding and accepting a purpose is "unscientific."

The sciences that deal with human behavior in society have likewise been enormously influenced by the mechanical model. The Newtonian paradigm has drawn economists and sociologists into the attempt to formulate laws analogous to the laws of classical physics, on the basis of which predictions could be made for the future. Armies of experts are employed by governments and business corporations in the belief that the future performance of human beings in their roles as consumers, producers, and citizens can be predicted and thus, by altering their circumstances, controlled. The recent advances in computer technology have stimulated further development into even more ambitious projects of futurology. It is not difficult to show both that this kind of prediction is—except to a very limited extent—theoretically impossible and also that in practice its failures are much more evident than its successes.[7]

If one takes the single most far-reaching change in the world of thought in this century, namely, the one associated with the name of Einstein, it is not only impossible to imagine that it could have been predicted in 1850; it is also absurd, because to have predicted it would have been already to achieve it. Once again, we have to say that whatever may be the usefulness of mechanical models in economics or sociology, these can in no way provide an explanation for human behavior, much less a way of predicting it.

In the first chapter I spoke of the characteristic dichotomy in our culture between a public world of "facts" and

7. See MacIntyre, *After Virtue,* pp. 84-102.

a private world of "values." Plainly, what I have been sketching in these recent paragraphs is what is called the world of facts, broadly conceived as a world of material entities operating according to laws that are mechanical in character. Corresponding to this world of facts is a kind of knowledge that is understood to be objective and impersonal, a knowledge that does not involve the knower in a personal risk. One may make the point simply by referring to the ways in which this knowledge is communicated in the course of the school curriculum. The statements of a textbook in physics, biology, or economics are not normally introduced by the phrase "I believe" or "we believe," as are the creedal statements of the church. The latter statements explicitly involve a personal commitment; by implication it is possible not to believe. The statements in a scientific textbook (and I am not speaking here of scientific papers written at the frontier of new discovery, where the real nature of scientific knowledge becomes explicit) are made in the third person, and there is no suggestion that the writer is at risk. Here we are dealing not with personal opinions but with facts.

It is at this point that we touch the central core of our culture, which is an ideal of knowledge of what are called "the facts," a knowledge that is supposed to be quite independent of the personal commitment of the knower. "Fact," says Alasdair MacIntyre, "is in modern western culture a folk-concept with an aristocratic ancestry."[8] The aristocrat involved was Lord Bacon, who advised his contemporaries to abjure speculation and collect facts. By speculation, he was referring to the Aristotelian belief that things are to be understood in terms of their end or purpose. This he rejected. But what resulted from his call was not the activity of a lot of magpies collecting any odds and ends lying about with no rhyme or reason. It was shaped—as any rational activity has to be shaped—by another speculative framework, namely, the belief that things are to be understood in terms of their causes. The "facts" thus understood are "value-free" insofar as the idea of value is related to an end or purpose for which the thing in

8. Ibid., p. 76.

question is or is not well fitted. Here is the origin of what MacIntyre calls the folk-concept of "fact" that dominates the consciousness of modern Western man. There is in this view a world of facts that is the real world, an austere world in which human hopes, desires, and purposes have no place. The facts are facts, and they are value-free. The personal beliefs and value judgments of the student do not enter into the picture. They have their place in another realm of discourse, in that area where the personal opinions, tastes, and convictions of individuals are freely exercised in a pluralistic society. There is no need for the writer of the science textbook to use the formula "I believe," because the facts are simply there whether one believes them or not. Science thus relieves one of the responsibility of deciding whether or not to commit himself to the truth of its statements. They are just facts.

And yet this folk-concept of a world of facts is denied by the actual practice of science. At the frontier of research, scientists do have to make difficult decisions whether or not to commit themselves to a new line of enquiry. They have to decide which problems are worth investigating and which are not. They have to make value judgments in the light of a vision of the purpose of scientific activity. The decision may make or break the scientist's career. And the scientist is sustained in his intense mental struggle by a passionate concern to solve the problem he has decided to tackle. His enterprise is not value-free: it is impregnated through and through by commitment to a purpose. And, to return to the school textbooks, even the humblest student beginning the study of physics engages in a purposeful activity. The facts described in the textbook do not simply imprint themselves on his mind. They have to be understood through an arduous enterprise of learning the appropriate skill in the use of words, of ideas, and of apparati. And this only happens if there is a preliminary act of faith—faith that the enterprise is worthwhile, that the methods developed by previous scientists are trustworthy, and that the teacher is a competent exponent of them.

So we already have the evidence of the dichotomy that

runs through our culture. We all engage in purposeful activity, and we judge ourselves and others in terms of success in achieving the purposes that we set before ourselves. Yet we accept as the final product of this purposeful activity a picture of the world from which purpose has been eliminated. Purpose is a meaningful concept in relation to our own consciousness of ourselves, but it is allowed no place in our understanding of the world of facts. Perhaps the point at which the self-contradiction becomes most obvious is in the application of social sciences to public administration. A social scientist who believes that he can understand and therefore predict and control human behavior on the basis of value-free scientific laws, that is, laws that do not assume any disputable judgments about what is good for human beings, is called upon to apply his skills as a civil servant. He cannot do so without acknowledging his capacity to pursue self-chosen purposes with a freedom that his science denies to those upon whom he is operating. The manipulator credits himself with the capacity for purposeful action that he denies to the manipulated. And if his purposes are questioned, there is no agreed-upon framework of "facts" by which they can be evaluated, for facts are value-free. It becomes simply a matter of the comparative skill and vigor of the different manipulators. If one goes on to ask, "By what criteria can the manipulator determine the direction in which to influence human behavior?" it will not be sufficient to answer with a recital of traditional moral values. These rest upon a different (and older) world-view and have no basis in "facts." Of course, most scientists are still influenced by their traditional values; but insofar as they wish to be rigorously consistent, these scientific manipulators cannot allow those values to be determinative. If they are eliminated, what will control the scientist's judgment? It can only be whatever element in his mental and emotional constitution is of greatest force. In eliminating purpose from the category of "facts," the manipulator hands over control to whatever is of predominant force in his own nature. Man's conquest of nature turns out to be nature's conquest of man.

We have again come, from another angle, to the cleavage running through our culture between the private and the public worlds, a public world interpreted in terms of efficient causes and a private world in which purpose and therefore value judgments still have a place. I have affirmed that we cannot accept the situation in which Christian faith is admitted as no more than a possible option for the private sector. We cannot settle for a peaceful coexistence between science and religion on the basis of an allocation of their spheres of influence to the public and the private sectors respectively. We cannot forever live our lives in two different worlds. We cannot forever postpone this question: What is the real truth about the world?

A missionary encounter with our culture must bring us face to face with the central citadel of our culture, which is the belief that is based on the immense achievements of the scientific method and, to a limited but increasing extent, embodied in our political, economic, and social practice—the belief that the real world, the reality with which we have to do, is a world that is to be understood in terms of efficient causes and not of final causes, a world that is not governed by an intelligible purpose, and thus a world in which the answer to the question of what is good has to be left to the private opinion of each individual and cannot be included in the body of accepted facts that control public life. We have to go back to the point where Lord Bacon advised his followers to collect facts and abjure speculation and ask exactly what is meant by *knowing* the facts.

Knowing is the exercise of a skill that has to be learned. It has to be learned by submitting to the authority of parents, teachers, and learned men and women, and giving our attention, often with some strain, to what they say. It is a purposeful activity in which we sometimes succeed and sometimes fail. It is not a mechanical process. Facts do not imprint themselves on our brains in the way that images of objects are imprinted on a photographic plate.

As learning proceeds, more and more of what we know passes from a conscious awareness to a kind of knowledge of which we are not directly aware. In learning to read, we have to begin by attending to the exact shape of the letters. Soon we can stop worrying about these and learn to recognize words. Later we are no longer aware of the individual words but take in the meaning of whole sentences and even paragraphs. If we habitually use different languages, we may remember what a paragraph said but forget what language it was in. Our knowledge of the whole depends on knowing the letters and words; yet as we read we are not aware of the knowledge. Polanyi takes this as an example of what he calls the tacit component in knowing. We can attend focally to the meaning of the paragraph because we are tacitly aware of the marks on the paper and the separate words. If, on the other hand, we are reading the proofs of a book, we have to attend focally to the words on the paper while tacitly being aware of the meaning of the whole.[9]

A very large part of our knowledge is tacit and cannot be communicated by specifying precise details. I can immediately recognize my wife in a crowd of a thousand people, but I could not give a description of her that would enable anyone else to do so. In this sense I know a great deal more than I can put into words. There are millions of human beings whose faces are basically formed in the same way and with the same color, but I could never confuse one of these with my wife. Yet I could not account for this fact by the most detailed measurements of her nose, chin, forehead, and so forth. This is the most vivid example of our capacity to recognize a configuration that is made up of many details. While we attend to the pattern we are only subsidiarily aware of the details. But a complete account of the details by itself would not enable us to recognize a pattern. This is why I said above that a person who knew everything specified in Laplace's formulas for perfect knowledge would in fact know nothing; for to know the smallest components of an entity is not to know the entity unless we also know the pattern, and our knowledge of patterns is much more than can be specified in words. Therefore, the Laplacean ideal, which still exercises such a determinative influence over

9. Polanyi, *Personal Knowledge,* esp. pp. 95-100.

popular understanding of science, can only lead into a blind alley.

All science develops by the recognition of significant patterns, and the power to recognize them is a skill that is developed only through practice. There are no mathematical rules for deciding whether any configuration is a significant pattern or is simply an accident. The statistical probability of a collection of pebbles falling into a significant pattern is precisely the same as the probability of their falling into any one particular random grouping. Our recognition of a significant pattern is an act of personal judgment for which there are no rules. It is a judgment of value: the pattern represents something a human being finds meaningful in terms of intrinsic beauty or of purpose. And although rules have been devised for quantifying the regularity in a series that may or may not be random, the application of these rules by the scientist to a particular case is a matter of personal judgment that depends on skills acquired by practice and is not capable of quantification or of verbal definition.[10]

One particularly clear example will enable us to move to the next stage of the argument. A machine is a collection of components that can be analyzed chemically into their elements and physically into the molecular and atomic particles that constitute them. Yet the most exhaustive chemical and physical analysis would not enable me to understand the machine unless I understood the purpose for which it was designed. As I have already remarked, it is, of course, possible to explain a particular component by speaking of its function within the total operation of the machine; and if the whole universe were to be conceived of as a vast mechanism, then each component part, including human beings, could be "explained" in terms of function. But since we have no knowledge of machines other than those devised and constructed by human beings to fulfill purposes entertained by the constructors, it is absurd to posit as the ultimate framework of explanation a machine constructed by nobody for no purpose.

In seeking to understand a machine, we employ the

10. From R. A. Fisher, *The Design of Experiments* (1935), quoted in Polanyi, pp. 22ff.

concepts of both efficient cause and final cause. If the machine breaks down because one of the components has been eroded by wear and tear, I could properly say that the cause of the breakdown was fully understood by referring to the physical and chemical processes that caused the erosion and therefore the breakdown. But when the machine is in proper working order, it would be absurd to say that the chemical and physical laws governing the structure and movement of its parts are the sufficient explanation of the machine. It can be explained only in terms of the purpose for which it has been constructed. Thus the physical and chemical laws can furnish a full explanation for the cause of failure, but a full explanation for the successful working of the machine cannot be given in terms of physics and chemistry but must be in terms of mechanics and must include an understanding of the purpose for which the machine is designed.[11]

From this example one can move to that of the animals, which are in some respects machinelike entities in that their bodies are composed of moving parts that can be understood only in terms of the purposes they serve. The difference here is that the purpose is internalized. A machine has no purpose of its own; it embodies the purpose of its designer. An animal—as innumerable experiments have demonstrated beyond the possibility of doubt—has purposes of its own. It has been shown that even earthworms are capable of learning from experience how to solve a problem. And animals closest to humans in intelligence, such as chimpanzees, are capable of identifying problems and developing very sophisticated strategies for solving them. Once again, as in the case of a machine, the physical and chemical constitution of animals' limbs and organs provides the necessary *conditions* for an animal's functioning, and if these deviate from the normal, the animal will fail and we shall rightly say that this physical or chemical event was the sufficient cause of the failure. But it would be absurd to say that either that or complete knowledge of the molecular activity in its organs constituted an explanation of the animal's behavior

---

11. See Polanyi, *Personal Knowledge,* pp. 331 ff.

apart from an understanding of the purposes it sets before itself, or that this molecular activity was the cause of the behavior as though there were no difference between a purposeful action and a jerk caused by the application of an electric shock to the nerves that activate the muscles.

At each level that we have been considering, we have seen that understanding requires the recognition both of detail and of overall pattern. All chemical reactions are conditioned by the molecular changes that are the subject of physics, but chemistry as a distinct discipline cannot be simply replaced by physics. All mechanical operations are conditioned by the chemical and physical operations of the component parts of the machine; but mechanics is still a necessary form of knowledge and cannot be replaced by physics and chemistry. All animal life is conditioned by the successful working of the limbs and organs, which is in turn conditioned by the laws of chemistry and physics and mechanics. But biology is still a proper study in its own right. The Laplacean ideal, which pretends that by a complete knowledge of the smallest elements we would know everything, is absurd. At each of these levels we are able to understand only because, while we focus attention on one level, our minds are operating with a vast amount of tacit awareness that has been gained by attention to other levels. In observing the behavior of an animal, we judge its success or failure in relationship to the purpose it is trying to achieve—to catch its prey, to build a nest, to protect its young, and so forth. Detailed knowledge of the mechanical, chemical, and—ultimately—atomic factors that condition success or failure is relevant to our understanding but is in no sense a substitute for it. It would be absurd to say that we understand the behavior of the bird engaged in building its nest by possessing a complete knowledge of the atomic and molecular changes in its tissues. We may for certain purposes attend focally to these precisely because we are aware of and are interested in the whole purposeful activity of building a nest.

I have sketched a series of levels of explanation stretching through physics, chemistry, and mechanics to biology.

At each point the principles established at the lower levels condition the higher level but do not explain it. At any level, the reductionist attempt to substitute a precise description of the components for an understanding of the whole fails. Physics cannot replace chemistry, nor chemistry mechanics, nor mechanics biology. We now have to move to the next level, namely, to our understanding of other human beings. Here the new factor entering in is the possibility of full, or at least growing, reciprocity. I use the word *full* to make the point that there can be a partial reciprocity at lower levels. A biologist observing the behavior of an earthworm is in a unidirectional relationship. The worm does not observe the biologist; there is no reciprocity. But a shepherd with his sheepdog is in a relationship in which there is real, though partial, reciprocity. No one can watch a Northumberland shepherd and his dog working together without acknowledging that a mutual understanding exists between them. So as we go up the scale, there are no absolute breaks. And I use the word *possibility* because it is, alas, possible for a practitioner of what are sometimes called the human sciences to regard his fellow human beings in the same way the biologist regards an earthworm. In the development of our scientific culture there have been essays in this direction. I shall not discuss them except to draw attention to the point that they represent the carrying of one of the fundamental assumptions of our culture to its logical conclusion. (This possibility forms the basis of C. S. Lewis's novel *That Hideous Strength.*)

Leaving this point aside, I come to the principles involved in the mutual understanding that can exist between two human beings. Each is aware of the other through the medium of a whole range of audiovisual impressions. As in the case of learning to read a written text, so in our learning to communicate with others from our earliest infancy, we have to learn to recognize gestures, expressions, words, intonations. Yet in a mature relationship we do not directly attend to any of these things. The audiovisual experiences condition our knowledge of the other person, but it would be absurd to say that they cause it, or that they explain it, or that we infer the existence of the person from these audiovisual data. They form part of the tacit knowledge that makes it possible to attend focally to the person, not as a physical or chemical or biological entity but as the subject of beliefs, experiences, and purposes similar to our own. Once again, this is nothing automatic. It is the fruit of a purposeful effort to understand, and it is evoked by the purposeful effort of the other party to communicate. The infant of a few weeks does not yet have the power of understanding fully developed. This power is evoked by the loving actions and gestures and words of mother and father, sisters and brothers, until he reaches the point in mature life where the relationship approaches full reciprocity.

If we ask what precisely is new in this reciprocal understanding between mature adults, as compared with, for example, the understanding between a shepherd and his dog, the answer must be somewhat as follows. A clever sheepdog quickly understands his master's purpose: it is to get that particular sheep separated from the flock and brought into this pen. The shepherd knows that the dog is tempted by other conflicting purposes, such as chasing a rabbit, but he simply overrules them. And even in this relationship the shepherd acts not by coercion but by the exercise of an authority the dog has learned to acknowledge. If it is anyone other than his own master, the dog will forget the sheep and go after the rabbit. Human beings have contrasting and sometimes conflicting purposes, but in a mature relationship one does not simply overrule the other. Of course, if A is a practitioner of social engineering or psychiatric manipulation, he may treat B's commitment to pacifism or to religious belief as simply a deviation that has to be corrected. He may also be able to identify the chemical, economic, or other factors that he regards as the sufficient cause of this deviation; and he may have techniques for rectifying them. We know that such a concept of human relations exists, but we recognize that it is different from a mature relationship in which A and B mutually acknowledge one another as responsible persons. In such a mature relationship there is no way of dealing with conflicts between differing purposes except by a process of mutual exchange, in which each tries to communicate to the other his perception of what is the proper objective of purposeful action, in other words, of what is good. In this context, the word *good* is obviously irrelevant if it means only "what I want for myself." It can only mean "good absolutely, good for all." If it does not mean this, the whole exercise in mutual communication is meaningless. If there is nothing that is "good" in this universal sense, then in every conflict of interest the only argument that is not meaningless is "this is what I want to do." And in that case the only possible way in which conflicting purposes can be reconciled to each other is for the strong to manipulate or coerce the weak. And, as we scarcely need to be reminded, modern technology has provided us with many sophisticated ways of doing this.

By contrast, in a mutual relationship between two mature human beings, we know that the relationship can be sustained only if we both acknowledge something that has authority over both and if each trusts the other to acknowledge this. In other words, I must treat the other person in accordance with the purpose for which (or whom) he or she exists and not as an object to be used for my purposes. But if, as seems to be the case, there are no absolute breaks in the continuity of being between humans, animals, plants, and inanimate objects, it would follow that, even with regard to subhuman beings, I am under obligation to respect the purpose for which they exist and am not free to subject them to my own. It need hardly be said that the implications of this for contemporary ecological issues, as well as for the ethics of a consumer society, are enormous.

Have we, in discussing the mutual relationships between mature human beings, reached the top of the hierarchy of ways of knowing? Obviously not, for in describing their relationships we have had to invoke the concept of "the good" as something both parties have to acknowledge as having authority, as that by which conflicting purposes have to be assessed. But what kind of knowledge could it be that gives knowledge of "the good"? Will it be by following Bacon's admonition and observing "the facts"? That would be to fall again into the reductionist trap. We do not understand the mind of another person by even the most painstaking examination of all the facts—physiological, psychological, biographical—about him or her. This kind of knowledge of the facts about a person can only be a subsidiary—and normally tacit—element in knowing the person as a person. Our ordinary language conveys very simply the sharp distinction that we draw between the most expert knowledge of the facts *about* a person and the experience of knowing that person. The sharpness of the distinction becomes clear when—as sometimes happens—a discussion of a person is interrupted by the sudden arrival of the person himself. The discussion has to be broken off altogether or else converted into a different kind of discussion in which we listen to the person himself speaking. Speech in the third person has to be replaced by speech in the first and second. In our normal speech we say that to carry on the former discussion about the person would be simply to ignore the person.

The same kind of break has to occur at this point in our discussion. It is the break that marks the limit of what is usually called natural theology. It is the same break as the one we met in the preceding chapter when I said that the model of the hermeneutical circle was not adequate for the interpretation of the Bible from outside the commitment of the believing community. I have suggested the ways in which the concept of purpose becomes more and more necessary as we ascend without a break through the realms of physics, chemistry, mechanics, and biology to the human person. I have reached a place where one could say that there are pointers to the fact that we cannot stop with the human level and that human conversation itself becomes inexplicable without reference to something beyond itself. And obviously, all of this argument is possible because I who argue and you who listen have already the experience of purposeful action. But no analysis of nature, from the lowest proton to the highest form of human life, could enable us to have direct knowledge of any purpose beyond our own. We do not infer the existence of another person from an analysis and classification of the audiovisual sensations we receive, but rather we attend directly to the person as a living center of meaning and purpose, and for this direct relationship our awareness of the sounds and gestures made by the other person is subsidiary and tacit. Thus it would also be idle to suppose that we could come to the knowledge of a supernatural personal reality by induction from all the data of our natural experience. At this point the only relevant questions are: Is there anyone present? Has he spoken? Natural theology ends here; another kind of enterprise begins, and another kind of language has to be used—the language of testimony.

The Christian church testifies that in the actual events of this finite, contingent, and yet rational world of warped space-time there are words and gestures through which the Creator and Sustainer of the world has spoken and acted. It is not that the events are anything other than part of the unbroken nexus of happenings within space-time that can be analyzed and classified along with all the rest. They are not "interventions" by someone who is otherwise absent. And—even more important—it is not that we are talking about something called religious experience as a separate form of cognition. That the word *religion* points to a kind of experience that is widely diffused throughout human history is an obvious fact. But that what is called religion is the only or the primary form of contact between the human race and its Creator is a mere assertion that has no logical foundation. It is simply one of the unexamined assumptions of our culture. As a member of the Christian church and from within its fellowship, I believe and testify (and the shift to the first person singular is, of course, deliberate) that in the body of literature we call the Bible, continuously reinterpreted in the actual missionary experience of the church through the centuries and among the nations, there is a true rendering of the character and purpose of the Creator and Sustainer of all nature, and that it is this character and purpose that determines what is good. Because I so believe and testify, I reject the division of human experience into a private world, where the "good" is a matter of personal taste, and a public world, where "facts" are regarded as operative apart from any reference to the good. I believe that all created beings have a sacramental character in that they exist by the creative goodness and for the redeeming purpose of God, that nothing is rightly understood otherwise, and that, nevertheless, God in creating a world with a measure of autonomy and contingency has provided for us a space within which we are given freedom to search, to experiment, and to find out for ourselves how things really are. I believe that the whole of experience in the natural world, in the world of public affairs, of politics, economics, and culture, and the world of inward spiritual experience is to be seen as one whole in the light of this disclosure of the character and will of its Creator.

As we came up the ladder from physics through chemistry, mechanics, and biology, to the understanding of the human person, we reached the point where we could speak of a mutual relationship between human beings approaching full reciprocity. We know that at the deepest levels of interpersonal relationships—of friend with friend, of man and woman in love—there is always the longing for complete mutual understanding. But we know that it is never in fact complete, and never wholly free from the danger that one subordinates the other, uses the other, manipulates the other. Can there ever be complete reciprocity, or is this an unattainable ideal to be striven for but never reached? Is it a mirage or a reality that can be reached?

The Christian testimony is that it is a reality within the being of the Triune God. This testimony rests on the fact that in a life lived as part of our human history, Jesus manifested a relationship of unbroken love and obedience to the one he called Father, a love and obedience sustained by the unfailing love and faithfulness of that same Father; and that those who believe and follow have been enabled through the presence of the Spirit actually to participate in this shared life of mutual love, which is the being of the Trinity, by being made one in the sonship of Jesus. This given reality of participation is most succinctly expressed in the words of the prayer attributed to Jesus by John: "The glory which thou hast given me I have given to them, that they may be one even as we are one, I in them and thou in me, that they may become perfectly one, so that the world may believe" (John 17:23). Here is the reality of a fully reciprocal relationship between the Father and the Son within the being of the Godhead, into which believers are drawn by the power of the Spirit, and out of which they can bear witness to the world of that reality from which all things proceed, for which all things exist, and by which all things are to be understood. It is a reality within which they can seek and summon others to seek that fully reciprocal understanding between persons that we can only approximate in this life but which we hope to attain fully in the life to come, when we shall know as we are known (1 Cor. 13:12).

The twin dogmas of Incarnation and Trinity thus form the starting point for a way of understanding reality as a whole, a way that leads out into a wider and more inclusive rationality than the real but limited rationality of the reductionist views that try to explain the whole of reality in terms of the natural sciences from physics to biology, a wider rationality that in no way negates but acknowledges and includes these other kinds of explanations as proper and necessary at their respective levels.

It is from this point of view that I can begin to understand and cope with a world that is both rational and contingent. For at the center of this disclosure, providing the clue to the whole, there stands the cross, on which the one whose purpose is the source and goal of all was slain in shame and dereliction, and the resurrection, in which that very death became the source of life. This precludes any shortcuts to meaningfulness that would ignore the radical contingency of things. The sort of immanent rationality that supposes that everything can be explained in mechanical, organismic, or mathematical terms is excluded, and so is whatever supposes (after the manner of some kinds of religion) that everything is controlled in the interests of the good as I conceive it. The meaningfulness of things seen in this light is compatible with the recognition of mystery that can only be borne in the course of a resolute following on the way of the cross. On the one hand, one is protected from a sheer irrationalism, for which there is no meaning in the world and everything is incomprehensible accident. On the other hand, following the way of the cross in the light and power of the resurrection, one is able to acknowledge and face the reality of evil, of that which contradicts God's good purpose, in the confidence that it does not have the last word. Here, in the responsible acceptance of this communication of a personal purpose of good, is the ground upon which it is possible to believe that the world is both rational and contingent.

Having made the break that was marked by my move into the language of testimony, I can now go back, so to speak, down the continuous ladder that connects human experience through the animal and plant world to the world of molecules, atoms, protons, and electrons. Coming up the ladder, we saw that at each stage the elements of the lower level condition but do not explain the higher. Coming down now from the top, with the faith that there is a good purpose that can be known through the data of experience in the space-time world, namely, those events that are the subject of the gospel message, we can see both why the category of purpose cannot be eliminated from our total understanding of how things are, and also—I suggest—how purpose may be recognized throughout the whole range of nature and not merely at the point where *homo sapiens* emerges. It is well known that, as a result of the demonstration of the noninheritability of acquired characteristics, evolutionary theory rejected Lamarkian ideas of purpose and accepted the Darwinian view that natural selection operates only on the results of random mutations. Recent discussion of the way natural selection works seems to leave room for the operation of purposeful activity as a factor in evolution, a factor that was excluded when all the emphasis was on the random mutation of genes. The discovery of the DNA molecule has altered the picture by showing that the limits of possible randomness are much smaller than was thought. And biologists now think in terms of populations sharing a pool of genes rather than of individuals, so that they are not dealing with the random behavior of individual units but with the behavior of very large numbers in which the randomness of individual units loses its importance. Moreover, there is more attention paid to the role of purpose in the ways by which animals adapt to their environment, which can play a role in the evolution of the species: "Characters acquired by individuals are not inherited by their individual offspring. But characters acquired by populations are inherited by their offspring populations if they are adaptive."[12]

It is obvious that in the case of *homo sapiens,* purposeful activity plays a central part in the business of adapting to environment. And, according to many biologists, this is also true of at least the higher forms of animal life. Parent birds and animals take great pains to initiate their young into the various strategies necessary for survival. It is hard to deny the parallel between this and the way the human infant is enabled to develop the powers of perception, comprehension, and communication and the skills necessary for coping with the environment. We develop into mature human beings not by an automatic process operating from within the human person as a separate organism but as a response to the cherishing and training of our parents and teachers. The process by which a human fetus eventually becomes a mature person able to recognize and follow what is good depends on the loving and purposeful will of those who have gone before. There is no logical break between this and the way a dog is trained to understand, love, and serve its master. It is not unreasonable to suggest that, since purpose plays this role in development at the point where we have the most intimate knowledge, it may play a part in some way right down to the lowest levels.

If we look at the picture of nature as a whole that modern science gives us, one of the puzzling facts is that while biology shows us the continuing evolution of more and more complex organisms, physics shows us—in the

---

12. C. H. Waddington, quoted in Thorpe, *Purpose in a World of Chance,* p. 34.

Second Law of Thermodynamics—a picture of relentless descent into entropy, into total randomness. The fundamental law of biology thus seems to operate in the opposite direction of the fundamental law of physics. I am aware of the work on what are called "dissipative structures," which has shown that, within a total context of increasing entropy, ordered patterns can spontaneously occur.[13] But it is difficult to see how this removes the perplexity. It shows that biological evolution is possible in terms of the laws of physics, but it is difficult to see how it can explain the fact that the whole story of biological evolution moves in a direction exactly opposite the movement of the physical universe taken as a whole. Is it too rash to suggest that the clue could be found in the fact that is familiar to us in human life and that we now find to be operative at least in the higher levels of animal life—the fact that life moves toward its proper completion not automatically by any purely mechanical or organic process but in response to a loving purpose, which draws out and makes actual powers that were otherwise only latent and potential.

If I understand correctly, what I am saying has affinities with the proposal made recently by Daniel Hardy and David Ford, who find in the work of Prigogine on "dissipative structures" support for their view that "the fundamental state of the universe is nonequilibrial"; that a state of total entropy is not the baseline for understanding the cosmos; that since God is a superabundant and overflowing source of new being, the universe is "an abundant allowance of space time and energy through which more abundance can happen."[14]

Whether or not there is anything of validity in these suggestions is something that must be left to others to discuss. What must, I believe, be affirmed with confidence can be put briefly in five propositions with which I conclude this chapter.

1. While the methodological elimination of final causes

---

13. See Peacocke, *Creation and the World of Science*, pp. 97-100, on the work of Prigogine et al.

14. See *Jubilate: Theology in Praise* (1984), p. 118.

from the study of nature has been immensely fruitful, the attempt to explain all that exists solely in terms of efficient cause leads to conceptual absurdity and to social tyranny.

2. To recognize the place of final causes in the understanding of the world must lead to these questions: Is anyone there? Is there a word? This is because purpose is a personal reality and can be known only if the person whose purpose it is chooses to communicate it.

3. The church exists to testify that there is someone, that he has spoken, and that we can begin to know his purpose and to direct our personal and public lives by it.

4. The church, therefore, in its missionary encounter with modern Western culture, has to be quite bold and unembarrassed in using the language of testimony, since this testimony, so far from being capable of validation by methods of modern science, provides itself with the foundation on which modern science rests, namely, the assurance that the world is both rational and contingent.

5. When the ultimate explanation of things is found in the creating, sustaining, judging, and redeeming work of a personal God, then science can be the servant of humanity, not its master. It is only this testimony that can save our culture from dissolving into the irrational fanaticism that is the child of total skepticism. It will perhaps be the greatest task of the church in the twenty-first century to be the bastion of rationality in a world of unreason. But for that, Christians will have to learn that conversion is a matter not only of the heart and the will but also of the mind.

5. What is to be done? The Dialogue with Politics

I am concerned in these inquiries to ask this central question: What would be involved in a genuinely missionary encounter between the gospel and our post-Enlightenment culture? In the preceding chapter I spoke about the encounter at the intellectual level with what forms the mental and spiritual heart of our culture—modern science. I was pursuing the question "What can be known, and how can it be known?" But the gospel concerns not only that question but also the question "What is to be done?" A missionary encounter impinges on not only the ideas and beliefs of a people but also on its ways of behaving. And these ways are, of course, not merely private and domestic but public and political. It is, indeed, impossible completely to separate these two, for it is the same person who is active in both. Consequently, missionaries have not hesitated, in their encounter with strange cultures, to attack forms of behavior, whether private or public, that they deemed incompatible with God's will revealed in Christ. Thus, in the Indian society which I know, missionaries have attacked such deeply entrenched elements of public life as caste, dowry, child marriage, and the immolation of widows. In Africa they have similarly thrown their weight against polygamy and the slave trade. What would an encounter of the gospel with our post-Enlightenment culture involve for the public arena—the political, economic, and social aspects of our life?

We have to deal at the outset with the claim that the gospel has nothing directly to say on these matters. There are loud voices that insist that the church has no business meddling with matters of politics and economics; that its business is with the eternal salvation of the human soul; and that if it undertakes to give ethical advice at all, it should be confined to advice about personal conduct. The gospel, these voices tell us, is about changing people, not about changing systems and structures. Let the church keep out of public affairs and mind its own business!

Many things could be said about this opinion from the long perspective of history, but I shall confine myself to three:

1. The claim that the church should not be involved in

politics is clearly in line with the post-Enlightenment division of human life into the public world of facts and the private world of values. As an optional set of values for the personal life, Christianity has freedom to compete with others and to win such place as its merits can secure for it. It cannot claim a place in the public world of politics, economics, and social administration; this must be governed by those who have the expert knowledge of the "facts." This is, of course, a view that would have astonished Christians living in an earlier period of the church's history. And there is no need to repeat here what I said in the preceding chapter about the mythological function the concept of "facts" performs in our contemporary culture.

2. The negative side of the claim, namely, that the church should not be involved in politics, arises from its positive claim, namely, that the proper business of the church is with the eternal salvation of the individual soul. Here we are dealing with a dichotomy that has been characteristic of a great deal of human religious thought but is notably absent from the Bible.

The idea that the real essence of what it is to be a human can be found only by stripping away the visible, external, contingent, historical elements of human life is very common in Indian religion and in the Greek thought within which much of the church's first systematic thinking was done. In this view, a human being is essentially an eternal soul dwelling for a time within a physical body, which is part of the world of nature and through which the person is tied by the bonds of physical and biological necessity to this visible and tangible world. There is thus a dichotomy running right through a human's whole experience between the eternal world, with which he has direct contact by way of his rational and spiritual being, and the world of the senses, with which—during the brief period of life on earth and as part of a biological and social group—he has fleeting relationships. Granted this dichotomy, the business of the church is not with the ephemeral world of outward happenings but with the eternal world of abiding spiritual realities.

3. But if one turns to the Bible from this world of thought, he finds it obvious that quite different assumptions reign about the nature of the human being. From its beginning and throughout, the Bible views the individual person realistically as someone always involved in relationships with other human beings and with the world of nature. The Bible is the story of these relationships. At the outset, it characterizes human nature created in the image of God as the mutuality of man and woman. From this beginning in the primal family, the story is about the relations within and between families, clans, nations. Of course, there is much in the Bible about what may be called the interior dimension of human existence, about that area of our experience where we are conscious of our aloneness, of our unsharable responsibilities, of the fact that, although we are part of an ongoing physical, biological, and social process, we also know that and by knowing it affirm our transcendence of it. Yet there is no attempt in the Bible to separate out this dimension of human experience and treat it as solely real. The point at which we are all tempted to do this is the point where we face the mystery of death, for death is the place at which the human subject parts company finally with the physical, biological, and social process of which he has been a part. Alone among animals, it seems, human beings are aware that death is a mystery, and therefore they make provision, often elaborate provision, for the respectful disposal of the dead body. It is remarkable that the ancient Israelites, apparently, had no belief that anything significant lay beyond death. God's purpose as they understood it was to be worked out among the living and their descendants here on the earth, not in a world beyond the grave.

It follows from this way of understanding what it is to be human that there is no separation of the inward and spiritual from the outward, visible, and social. The Torah of Yahweh, his loving guidance and instruction for his people, concerns the whole of their life as persons, as families, and as a nation. Faith, obedience, repentance, and love are not bracketed off under the category of religion; on the contrary, they are embodied in ways of behaving that cover much of what we would describe as jurisprudence, public health, education, welfare, and economic policy. It is a simple fact, familiar to all who read the Bible, that if we want to read only the passages that are exclusively about what we call the spiritual life, we have to leave the greater part of the Old Testament unread.

What I am saying, of course, is familiar and usually leads to the assertion that we must read the Old Testament in the light of the New, and that when we do so, we shall see that the teachings of Jesus were not about these external and ephemeral things but about the eternal realities of the spirit, and that what is written in the Old Testament is to be read solely in that light. I want to say, however, that this spiritualizing of the teachings of the Old Testament does not do justice to the actual content of the New.

The message of Jesus was that the kingdom or reign of God is at hand. Behind it lay the faith of the Old Testament that while Yahweh had chosen one people to live under his Torah and so to be a witness to the nations, a day would come when all the nations would come to acknowledge him as God alone and live under his Torah. In addition, behind it lay the later molding of this faith into its apocalyptic form under the terrible pressure of successive disasters. As generations of faithful Israelites died martyrs' deaths in the struggle against the enemies of Yahweh, the old lack of interest in what lay beyond death gave way to a belief that the victory of Yahweh would bring along with it those who had given their lives for his sake. The victory of Yahweh would be his own work, bringing the present order to an end and establishing a new order in which those who had died in faith would also share. It is against the background of this apocalyptic expectation that we have to understand Jesus' message of the imminence of the reign of God.

As we well know, this apocalyptic expectation, without which we cannot understand the message of Jesus, was also the cause of misunderstanding. The story of the ministry as unfolded in the Synoptic Gospels shows us an initial enthusiasm gradually turning into unbelief and rejection as it became clear that the reign of God is a profoundly mysterious and paradoxical reality, which only a few chosen witnesses can understand. The victory of God is finally accomplished in the rejection and death of Jesus. The king reigns from the tree. That fact, hidden from the world, is proclaimed to those chosen as witnesses (and only to those) by the resurrection of Jesus from the dead. Those witnesses are sent forth to proclaim and to embody in their common life the victory of Jesus, the reality of the reign of God. They are to go, bearing about in their body the dying of Jesus, that the life of Jesus—the life of the victorious kingdom—may be made manifest in their bodily life (2 Cor. 4:10). They proclaim and embody the victory of God under the sign of the Cross.

Thus a new reality is brought into being, a new kind of human community in which the Torah of Yahweh is being fulfilled by people not only from the tribes of Israel but from all the nations. The promise of the prophets and the psalmists is being fulfilled. The nations are coming to the new Zion to be the people of Yahweh and to live under his rule, his Torah. They have become—from many races and nations—one family bound to one another in the brotherly relationships, the kinship bonds that were characteristic of the household of Israel in God's intention. They are no longer strangers to each other, but brothers and sisters; they are, as Israel was, one household—but drawn from all nations.

Thus the earliest church never availed itself of the protection it could have had under Roman law as a *cultus privatus* dedicated to the pursuit of a purely personal and spiritual salvation for its members. Such private religion flourished as vigorously in the world of the Eastern Mediterranean as it does in North America today. It was permitted by the imperial authorities for the same reason that its counterparts are permitted today: it did not challenge the political order. Why, then, did the church refuse this protection? Why did it have to engage in a battle to the death with the imperial powers? Because, true to its roots in the Old Testament, it could not accept relegation to a private sphere of purely inward and personal religion. It knew itself to be the bearer of the promise of the reign of Yahweh over all nations. It refused the names by which the many religious societies called themselves, and which critics such as Celsus applied to the church (*thiasos, hieranos*); it called itself the *ecclesia tou theou,* the public assembly to which God is calling all men everywhere without distinction. This made a collision with the imperial power inevitable—as inevitable as the Cross.[1]

But the church did not set out to create a new political order, or to take political action for the reformation of political institutions. It would be both anachronistic and theologically confused to infer that. The God-given—and therefore limited—authority of Caesar is acknowledged in the Bible (John 19:11). Pilate has God-given authority to pass judgment on Jesus, but Jesus is king in the absolute sense that he bears witness to the truth; the ultimate reality against which all kingship is to be measured is present in him (John 18:37). And when, as in this case, the God-given authority of a political order is placed at the service of a lie, a head-on collision is the only possible result. In the Cross the ruler of this world is unmasked and dethroned, and this decisive event is the clue to all subsequent history. The apocalyptic passages of the New Testament are the projection through history of the conflict that was fought out on the cross. In the end, the present order will pass away and Jesus will reign.

But how is the kingship of Christ exercised in the interim? While the church is a small minority living under an imperial power, the kinds of questions that arise in a modern democracy are obviously excluded. The church, in the power of the crucified and risen Jesus, bears witness to the truth and pays the price with its blood. But what was the church to do when the imperial power lost its will to continue and the emperor turned to the church to provide the spiritual cohesion for a disintegrating society? Much has been written about the harm done to the cause of the gospel when Constantine accepted baptism, and it

---

1. See G. Kittel, *Theological Dictionary of the New Testament*, s.v. "Ecclesia."

is not difficult to expatiate on this theme. But could any other choice have been made? When the ancient classical world, which had seemed so brilliant and so all-conquering, ran out of spiritual fuel and turned to the church as the one society that could hold a disintegrating world together, should the church have refused the appeal and washed its hands of responsibility for the political order? It could not do so if it was to be faithful to its origins in Israel and in the ministry of Jesus. It is easy to see with hindsight how quickly the church fell into the temptations of worldly power. It is easy to point—as monks and hermits, prophets and reformers in all ensuing centuries have continued to point—to the glaring contradiction between the Jesus of the Gospels and his followers occupying the seats of power and wealth. And yet we have to ask, would God's purpose as it is revealed in Scripture have been better served if the church had refused all political responsibility, if there had never been a "Christian" Europe, if all the churches for the past two thousand years had lived as tolerated or persecuted minorities like the Armenians, the Assyrians, and the Copts? I find it hard to think so.

Whatever one may think—and it is perhaps meaningless to engage in these speculations—two facts are fundamental to an understanding of our present situation. One is that we are the heirs of the Christendom experiment. We who belong to the Western world live in societies that have been shaped by more than a thousand years during which the barbarous and savage tribes of Europe were brought, slowly and with many setbacks, into a community conceived as the *corpus Christianum,* a single society in which the whole of public and private life was to be controlled by the Christian revelation. Much of what we take for granted about normal human behavior is the fruit of that long schooling. However much we rebel against it, we are its products.

The second fact is that the *corpus Christianum* is no more, and we cannot go back to it. The religious wars of the seventeenth century marked the final destruction of Christendom's synthesis of church and society. From the eighteenth century onward, Europe turned away from the

Christian vision of man and his world, accepted a radically different vision for its public life, and relegated the Christian vision to the status of a permitted option for the private sector. But for the modern church to accept this status is to do exactly what the early church refused to do and what the Bible forbids us to do. It is, in effect, to deny the kingship of Christ over all of life—public and private. It is to deny that Christ is, simply and finally, the truth by which all other claims to truth are to be tested. It is to abandon its calling.

The Enlightenment's vision of the heavenly city has failed. We are in a new situation, and we cannot turn back the clock. It is certain that we cannot go back to the *corpus Christianum*. It is also certain—and this needs to be said sharply in view of the prevalence among Christians of a kind of anarchistic romanticism—that we cannot go back to a pre-Constantinian innocence. We cannot use the example of the early church to encourage us in a Manichaean attempt to treat all power as evil and to wash our hands of responsibility for the realities of political power. We cannot go back on history. But perhaps we can learn from history. Perhaps we can learn how to embody in the life of the church a witness to the kingship of Christ over all life—its politic and economic no less than its personal and domestic morals—yet without falling into the Constantinian trap. That is the new, unprecedented, and immensely challenging task given to our generation. The resolute undertaking of it is fundamental to any genuinely missionary encounter of the gospel with our culture.

In order to view this task in some historical perspective, I would like to go back to Augustine, who, in his greatest work written near the end of his life, painted a picture of the relationship between church and world that was to shape the thought and practice of Western Christendom for a thousand years. It would have been equally relevant to refer to Augustine in the discussion of the interface between theology and science; for it was Augustine, standing at the point of collapse of the classical worldview, who inaugurated a new approach to knowledge with the slogan *credo ut intelligam*.[2] He provided a new basis

---

2. M. Polanyi, *Personal Knowledge*, pp. 266ff.

for critical thinking in the acceptance by faith of the twin dogmas of the Trinity and the Incarnation. I believe that Augustine's example is relevant to our situation today as we face a growing disillusionment about the modern scientific world-view. But here I am inviting attention to another facet of Augustine's achievement. When the inward and spiritual disintegration of the classical world-view was matched in the realm of outward and visible events by Alaric's sack of the Eternal City, and Augustine found his provincial diocese flooded with refugees—pagan and Christian—from Rome, he set himself as an old man his greatest task, the interpretation of secular history in the light of the gospel.

At Augustine's writing, a century had passed since Christians first sat on the imperial throne. Christians and pagans were mingled at all levels of public life. The church was not being persecuted, nor had the kingdom of God arrived in its fullness. Christians were scattered throughout the world as *peregrini,* a word which, properly translated, means not "pilgrims" but "resident aliens."[3] They had citizenship in another country. Thus citizens of two commonwealths were living commingled in each place: one, the earthly commonwealth, was ruled by the love of self, the other by the love of God. The latter was identified, if not exactly with the Catholic Church, then with those among its members who were truly governed by love for God. Augustine was very realistic about the evils that tear all human communities apart—the family, the city, the nation. In *The City of God* he has no sentimental illusions about natural brotherhood among human beings. Yet he insists that love is the basis of society; even in their wars men are in fact speaking peace.[4] But peace is only possible when there is order, and order depends on proper government; but government in which one is subordinated to another is only right if the one who is called to govern does so for the sake of those he governs—as their servant. The motive power of order is therefore love. Augustine's concept of human society is not based on a

3. See Peter Brown, *Augustine of Hippo,* p. 323.
4. *City of God,* XIX, 5-7, 12.

conception of justice drawn from elsewhere, for example, from natural law. Love, not natural justice, is what holds even the earthly commonwealth together. Thus

> God, the Instructor, teaches two main laws, love of God and love of one's neighbour. Here man finds three beings to love, God, himself and his neighbour. He who loves God makes no mistake in loving himself. Consequently, since he is ordered to love his neighbour as himself, he advises his neighbour also to love God. . . . He wishes to be similarly cared for by his neighbours if need arise. So far as in him lies he will be at peace with all men in that ordered harmony which is the peace of men.[5]

Thus love creates order first in the family and among neighbors and then, by extension, in the city and the nation. Without this, even the earthly commonwealth cannot exist. It is love that creates justice.

> Where that kind of justice does not exist—the kind in which the one Almighty God rules over an obedient city by his grace, in which no one sacrifices to any but him, in which on that account for all who belong to that city and obey God the mind faithfully rules the body, and the reason the vices, in proper order, and in which the assembly and people of just men live like one just man, that is to say by faith which works by love and by which a man loves God as he should be loved, and his neighbour as himself—where there is not that kind of justice there is certainly no society of men by consent of law or community of mutual service. If that is a true definition of a people, it follows that where such justice does not exist, there is no people. Therefore there is no republic, because there can be no commonwealth where there is not a people.[6]

Faith working through love is the foundation of justice, and without justice there is no commonwealth.

It follows that, like the exiles whom Jeremiah urged to seek the peace of Babylon, and like the early Christians who were urged to pray for kings and rulers, those who—as citizens of the city of God—are resident aliens in the earthly city, must nevertheless seek its good order, and,

---

5. Ibid., XIX, 14.
6. Ibid., XIX, 23.

when called to responsibility as rulers, must accept it in the spirit of servants of the common good. This is required by obedience to the law of God, which is love. Thus the citizens of the heavenly city will actively seek the peace and good order of the earthly city, not seeking to forestall, but patiently awaiting, the final judgment when the two will be visibly separated and the heavenly city will appear in all its beauty. Meanwhile, the monastic communities, such as the one to which Augustine belonged, are a visible sign and preliminary realization of a world ruled solely by the love of God in the midst of a world ruled by the love of self.

Such was the vision that controlled the relationship of church and society in the western part of Europe for the thousand years from the death of Augustine. The public world of government, of education, of buying and selling, of ruling and serving, was to be shaped so far as possible by the vision of an order in which love is expressed through the relations proper to a hierarchical order of which God, who is the source of all love, is the head. There are no illusions about the reality of sin that always threatens this order. But the greater reality is the sovereign Creator and Judge, who will at the end separate forever the just from the unjust, and justice will be equal, whether for peasant or pope.

Yet throughout the thousand-year period this order was challenged over and over again by movements that drew their inspiration from the apocalyptic strands of biblical and postbiblical writings. These writings voiced the anger and despair of those who saw the contrast between the gospel of Jesus and the worldliness of the church, and who again and again announced the imminent destruction of the present order and the arrival of the heavenly Jerusalem. In Norman Cohn's fascinating account of the millenarian movements that erupted throughout this period, the first of his examples dates from a mere 150 years after the death of Augustine.[7] There is a continuous line of such movements stretching through the people's crusades, the flagellants, the brethren of the Free Spirit,

---

7. N. Cohn, *The Pursuit of the Millennium.*

the Taborites of Bohemia, and the peasants' revolts, to the messianic reign of John of Leyden in Münster and the Ranters in England. In every case the vision they express is of the total disappearance of the existing political, economic, and ecclesiastical order and its replacement by some sort of theocracy—whether of a semidivine emperor or of the elect saints. And it is not difficult to see that the same line continues through the intellectual crisis of the Enlightenment and reappears in the heavenly city of the eighteenth-century philosophers, which has been so well described by Carl Becker in his book of that title.[8] In the course of the nineteenth century that view developed into the twin visions that have dominated the twentieth century: the liberal capitalist dream of inevitable progress toward a more and more enlightened, liberated, and happy world; and the Marxist dream of the apocalypse of freedom in a cataclysm that would abolish both private property and the state and create a society of perfect harmony.

We are at a time when both of those visions have faded. It can be claimed (as Langdon Gilkey has) that the only convinced Marxists today are the dissidents in the West, and the only convinced liberals are the dissidents in the East. In spite of the conflict between them, the two ideologies that officially operate on the two sides of the Iron Curtain have this in common: they are both atheist. The one attempts without success to enforce atheism in the private as well as the public sector. The other permits belief in God as an option for private life but excludes it from any controlling role in public life. We have to look briefly at the steps by which Christendom moved from the medieval assumption that economics is part of ethics and therefore depends upon theology, to the modern assumption that economics is an autonomous science with which theology has nothing to do.

R. H. Tawney's classic study *Religion and the Rise of Capitalism* shows that the Reformers—both Lutheran and Calvinist—continued to take it for granted that a Christian is governed by the law of God in his economic life as

---

8. C. Becker, *The Heavenly City of the Eighteenth-Century Philosophers* (1967).

much as in any other activity. Luther regarded the rising capitalism of fifteenth- and sixteenth-century Germany as a work of the devil, maintained intact the traditional teaching that absolutely forbade interest on loans, and condemned as sin the selling of goods for the highest price they would bear. But, characteristically, he made no attempt to revise the medieval casuistry to bring it into touch with the new economic facts; it was enough that the man set free by grace would learn how to love his neighbor in all the practical affairs of life by consulting Scripture and his conscience. Calvin, on the other hand, much closer than Luther to the economic forces that were changing the nature of European society, recognized that credit is a necessary element in the growth of commerce and industry. He thus allowed a reasonable interest on loans for this purpose but in no way altered the ancient doctrine that all such activity is subject to the law of God. Accepting urban society, with its trade and industry, Calvin sought to create a civic society in which every sort of activity — political, economic, or cultural — was controlled in accordance with the purpose of all human life as set forth in Scripture, namely, the glory of God and the salvation of men and women. Neither for Luther nor for Calvin would it have appeared as anything other than incomprehensible blasphemy to suggest that human behavior in the sphere of economics was outside the jurisdiction of theology. On the contrary, buying and selling, hiring labor and working for a master, amassing wealth and enclosing land — these are precisely the human activities in greatest need of the reminder that every man stands under the law of God and will be accountable to God for his treatment of his neighbor.

Of course, there has never been a time when it was easy to keep this in mind; but there were forces at work in the fifteenth and sixteenth centuries that made it more than ordinarily difficult. The Black Death's devastation had disrupted feudal society. The discovery of the New World was flooding Europe with silver and gold and producing a huge inflation of prices, destroying the ancient balance in society, and making possible a vast extension of trade to the far corners of the earth. Old rules governing wages, prices, interest, and land tenure became impossible to maintain. Capital was no longer primarily the adjunct of the labor of the small craftsman; it became more and more the master that controlled economic organization.

Through the sixteenth and seventeenth centuries, Protestant divines continued to insist that the writ of Christ ran in all the working of economics: they denounced the amassing of capital, the enclosure of lands, and the oppression of the poor. And some, such as William Law and John Wesley, carried the same teaching into the eighteenth century. But other forces were at hand to provide armor for the cupidity of the natural man against the thunder of a preacher like Luther or the calm advice of a pastor like Richard Baxter. One was a development of Calvinism itself; the other came from the new philosophy and science of Descartes and Newton. The Puritan development of Calvinism took over from Geneva both the assumption that economic activity falls under the rule of God and also the reformer's great emphasis on the personal responsibility of every Christian to manifest the reality of his calling and election by a life of hard work, self-denial, order, and rigorous discipline. These were the qualities that led to success in the new and expanding world of trade and industry in seventeenth-century Europe. Thus it happened (and this, of course, is an oft-repeated statement) that many of Calvin's most successful later followers forgot the strict limits he had drawn around economic activity and (to quote Tawney) added a "halo of ethical sanctification to the appeal of economic expediency"—with results that the Geneva Consistory would certainly not have approved.

But the other force I have referred to was more enduring and is much more significant today. It was and is the view of human affairs that found its inspiration in what the philosophers of the Enlightenment called "the geometrical spirit," which saw in the physics of Newton the true model for the explanation of all things, and which therefore sought to understand economics not in terms of man's chief end but in terms of laws that could be stated in mathematical and mechanical forms. Sir William Petty, author of the influential work *Political Arithmetic* in 1690, defined its objective as follows: "To express itself in terms of numbers, weight or measure, to use only arguments of sense, and to consider only such causes as have visible foundations in nature; leaving those that depend upon the mutable minds, opinions, appetites, and passions of particular men to the consideration of others." Here we have, of course, an early setting forth of that elimination of purpose as a category of explanation, that determination to seek all explanation in universally acknowledged natural causes, and that separation of a world of public facts from a world of personal values with which we are now familiar.

The autonomous science of economics was thenceforth to develop on the basis of the assumption that self-interest is a universal, natural, and calculable force analagous in this realm to the forces of gravity and inertia in the realm of physics, and that consequently it is possible to develop a science of economics that will be as mathematical and as independent of theology as is the physics of Newton. And since, for the eighteenth century, nature has taken the place of God and has inherited his benevolent character, it follows that the pursuit of self-interest will coincide with the purpose of God. Alexander Pope, as usual, concisely sums up the faith of his age:

> Thus God and Nature formed the general frame
> And bade self-love and social be the same.

Traditional Christian ethics had attacked covetousness as a deadly sin, and Paul had equated it with idolatry: the putting of something that is not God in the place belonging to God (Col. 3:5). The eighteenth century, by a remarkable inversion, found in covetousness not only a law of nature but the engine of progress by which the purpose of nature and nature's God was to be carried out.

The enormous consequences that have followed from this reversal of traditional values are familiar to us. It has shattered the age-long assumption that the world we inhabit is basically stable and finite and that consequently economics is mainly about the sharing of limited resources. It has shifted the focus of attention from distribution to production. It has made us familiar with the idea of ceaseless and limitless growth, of unending possibilities of increased mastery over nature that provides increased resources of food, materials, and energy. This is a world in which economics is mainly about increasing production, and it is assumed that if everyone pursues his rational self-interest, production will grow and distribution will take care of itself. Two hundred years after the Enlightenment, we live in a world in which millions of people enjoy a standard of material wealth that few kings and queens could have matched then, but in which the gulf between the rich minority and the abjectly poor majority is vast and growing, a world therefore threatened as never before by destructive violence. In protest against the injustices of unrestrained free-market capitalism, the Marxist creed holds out the hope of an apocalypse in which the dispossessed will seize power, the oppressors will perish, and all will live forever in perfect harmony. As that vision recedes farther and farther into the future, the Marxist states seek to combine the dynamism of modern science with a state control of economic activity designed to secure some equality in the distribution of wealth. In the quest for equality they sacrifice individual freedom, as capitalist states in the name of freedom sacrifice equality. Yet neither system can survive except by modifying the rigor of its ideology. All Marxist governments have to give some place to free-market enterprise, and all capitalist governments have to use state power to limit the injustices that unrestrained free-market enterprise creates.

Meanwhile, each side portrays the other as the very incarnation of evil, and the self-righteous fury of their ideological warfare threatens us for the first time in human history with the annihilation of the human race. The eighteenth-century philosophers turned from the Christian vision of a city that would come down from heaven to the enterprise of building the heavenly city on earth. That radical apostasy has now brought us to the place where we face another kind of apocalypse, the threat of global annihilation and the extinction of the human species.

Yet the biblical and classical Christian belief that the rule of Christ extends to all of life has never been totally extinguished. Christian faith has not only inspired programs for the relief of the victims of unrestrained capitalism both through welfare legislation and through voluntary work for sufferers, but it has also inspired ventures for the restructuring of economic life. Non-Marxist Christian socialism has an honorable history with real achievement to its credit. The Roman Catholic Church has continued to insist on its right and duty to make ethical judgments in economic affairs and—especially since the rise of the ecumenical movement—the non-Roman churches, through national and world bodies, have been active in doing the same. At the present time we are witnessing a strong countermovement that either asserts that churches have no right to meddle in matters of economics or—as in Michael Novak's *The Spirit of Democratic Capitalism*—boldly claims that capitalism is the form of economic organization that Christians must espouse. A brief look at Novak's position will bring us to the heart of our present discussion.

Novak takes as fundamental the separation of three elements of public life: the political, the economic, and the moral-cultural. These are separate realms, and any attempt of one to exercise control of the others will be disastrous. In the economic realm the basic law is that the free operation of rational self-interest will alone secure general well-being. Medieval ideas of a just price and fair wage were relevant to a static economy but are positively damaging to an economy of growth. Each person must be free to better his condition as far as he can, and he alone is the judge of what is better. There can be no imposed or even generally accepted norm of what is good. In the world of economic values "the central shrine is empty," for no image is adequate to express what is ultimately good.[9] Any attempts to subordinate economics to ethics would bring us back to the clerical control from which we

9. M. Novak, *The Spirit of Democratic Capitalism,* pp. 53-54.

had to escape in order to achieve growth; and any generally accepted vision of social order is a violation of transcendence.[10] But alongside the economic order is the moral-cultural order. Novak does not tell us what, if any, is the image in the central shrine here, but over and over again he tells us that the proper working of capitalism requires conscientious behavior in all concerned. "Capitalism," he tells us, "depends upon a moral-cultural system separate from the state."[11] Capitalism, he goes on to say, "needs strong moral guidance." And the family, where moral values are nourished, has therefore inalienable rights in a capitalist society. But to say that capitalism requires a certain kind of moral foundation is to say that capitalism cannot survive permanently in a purely secular society. To quote a recent writer, "The disinterested devotion which was vital to the creation of the capitalist world order and to the public life of industrial nations and which rested on a religious idea-system appears as a type of moral capital debt which is no longer being serviced."[12] But this means that capitalism cannot be a self-sustaining system. It depends on the moral-cultural system and cannot be separated from it. But moral imperatives cannot operate merely as useful props for a profitable economic order. If they are not rooted in some belief about how the universe is in fact ordered, they collapse; and if they are so rooted, then the economic order cannot be isolated from their jurisdiction. If capitalism depends on the insights of a moral conscience, then that conscience has to have authority over the working of capitalist economics.

Novak's argument thus seems to be both incoherent and—where it is coherent—anti-Christian. Its incoherence lies on the surface. The conscience that is required to keep capitalism going has no ontological basis. It is a carry-over from an earlier world-view. It is a fragment, a broken piece left over from the destruction of the older

---

10. Ibid., p. 70.
11. Ibid., p. 85.
12. B. Wilson, quoted in Habgood, *Church and Nation in a Secular Age*, p. 47.

view, preserved for the purpose of keeping the new system going. But moral imperatives only retain their power as part of a living system of belief, some vision of what is the case. Moral imperatives cannot be hired to prop up a wholly different set of values. As Jacques Maritain has said, "The sorest disasters can result in the life of a people when [morality] instead of acting as consubstantial with politics, essays to act on them from without, i.e., in the imposition of apolitical moral values on an amoral conception of politics."[13] A conscience that is forbidden to operate in the choice of goals for economic activity is not conscience in the sense in which any moralist, pagan or Christian, has ever understood the term. And the family (which Novak regards as vital to the spirit of democratic capitalism) is precisely the place where the noncapitalist values have to be learned, where one is not free to choose his company and where one is not free to pursue self-interest to the limit. Because capitalism pursues the opposite goals—the freedom of each individual to choose and pursue his own ends to the limit of his power—the disintegration of marriage and family life is one of the obvious characteristics of advanced capitalist societies. And insofar as Novak's argument is coherent, it is anti-Christian. To say that the central shrine is empty is to deny the Incarnation.

The driving power of capitalism, as Novak correctly emphasizes, is the desire of the individual to better his material condition. It is the unleashing of this power from the restraints imposed by traditional Christian morality that has transformed static societies into the dynamic and growing society of which we are a part. No one can deny either the reality of the motive force or the magnitude of what it has achieved. The name the New Testament gives to the force in question is covetousness. The capitalist system is powered by the unremitting stimulation of covetousness. The apostolic advice that a person should be content with food and clothing (1 Tim. 6:8) is not compatible with the development of our kind of society, and it would be better to acknowledge that frankly, as Novak

---

13. J. Maritain, *True Humanism,* p. 214.

does. The shrine has to be vacated if capitalism is to flourish. Modern capitalism has created a world totally different from anything known before. Previous ages have assumed that resources are limited and that economics—housekeeping—is about how to distribute them fairly. Since Adam Smith, we have learned to assume that exponential growth is the basic law of economics and that no limits can be set to it. The result is that increased production has become an end in itself; products are designed to become rapidly obsolete so as to make room for more production; a minority is ceaselessly urged to multiply its wants in order to keep the process going while the majority lacks the basic necessities for existence; and the whole ecosystem upon which human life depends is threatened with destruction. Growth is for the sake of growth and is not determined by any overarching social purpose. And that, of course, is an exact account of the phenomenon which, when it occurs in the human body, is called cancer. In the long perspective of history, it would be difficult to deny that the exuberant capitalism of the past 250 years will be diagnosed in the future as a desperately dangerous case of cancer in the body of human society—if indeed this cancer has not been terminal and there are actually survivors around to make the diagnosis.

But I should also acknowledge that many of Novak's criticisms of socialism are convincing. It is true that socialists, Christian socialists not excepted, tend to judge capitalism by actual practice but socialism by an ideal that has never yet been put into practice anywhere. There is a pathetic catalogue of socialist regimes that have been hailed one after another as models for the Christian to emulate and then found to be full of all kinds of corruptions and illusions. Novak is quite right to describe a great deal of Christian socialism as, in the strict sense, utopian. It is the politics of nowhere.

The debate between the capitalism of the so-called free world and the socialism of the Soviet Union and its allies has become as intellectually barren as it is practically perilous. Each side can point with devastating effect to the failures of the other, but each becomes ridiculous when it tries to conceal its own. Both parties have exhausted their moral and intellectual capital. But a genuinely missionary encounter of the gospel with our culture can go behind this futile and infinitely dangerous conflict to challenge the common beliefs on which both sides rely, beliefs that have long been regarded as axiomatic but are in fact false. Of course, as contemporary history proves, Christians can live and bear witness under any regime, whatever its ideology. But Christians can never seek refuge in a ghetto where their faith is not proclaimed as public truth for all. They can never agree that there is one law for themselves and another for the world. They can never admit that there are areas of human life where the writ of Christ does not run. They can never accept that there are orders of creation or powers or dominions that exist otherwise than to serve Christ. Whatever the institutional relationship between the church and the state—and there are many possible relationships, no one of which is necessarily the right one for all times and places—the church can never cease to remind governments that they are under the rule of Christ and that he alone is the judge of all they do. The church can never accept the thesis that the central shrine of public life is empty, in other words, that there has been no public revelation before the eyes of all the world of the purpose for which all things and all peoples have been created and which all governments must serve. It can never accept an ultimate pluralism as a creed even if it must—as of course it must—acknowledge plurality as a fact. In fact, it cannot accept the idea, so popular twenty years ago, of a secular society in which, on principle, there are no commonly acknowledged norms. We know now, I think, that the only possible product of that ideal is a pagan society. Human nature abhors a vacuum. The shrine does not remain empty. If the one true image, Jesus Christ, is not there, an idol will take its place. It is not difficult to name the idolatry that controls our culture; Paul has already done so. On the other hand, there can be no return to the era of the *corpus Christianum,* of the identification of the church with the ruling power. In this respect the movement of the Enlightenment is irreversible. We are indeed witnessing an attempt to restore a kind of society analagous to the *corpus Christianum* in the contemporary world of Islam. What is happening in Iran today has much to teach us. Why do the present leaders of that country denounce America and Russia equally as the agents of Satan? Because they have seen the fabric of their own society, its family life, its sexual ethics, and its ideas of what human life is for disintegrating under the influence of ideas coming through both these channels that stem from the European Enlightenment. We can understand and even sympathize, but we cannot follow. Islam denies the Christian doctrine of original sin and therefore believes that it is possible to achieve a total identification of the laws of a state with the law of God. Church and state in Islamic thought are one, without distinction of function. That way we cannot go. The sacralizing of politics, the total identification of a political goal with the will of God, always unleashes demonic powers.

We are witnessing the same thing, but under Christian auspices, in the emergence of what is called "the Religious Right" in the United States. The leaders of this movement, while accepting the biblical doctrine regarding the radical corruption of human nature by sin, in effect exempt themselves as "born-again Christians" from its operation. They identify their own cause unconditionally with the cause of God, regard their critics as agents of Satan, and are apparently prepared to see the human race obliterated in an apocalyptic catastrophe in which the nuclear arsenal of the United States is the instrument of Jesus Christ for the fulfillment of his purpose against the Soviet Union as the citadel of evil. This confusion of a particular and fallible set of political and moral judgments with the cause of Jesus Christ is more dangerous than the open rejection of the claim of Christ in Islam, just as the shrine of Jereboam at Bethel was more dangerous to the faith of Israel than was the open paganism of her neighbors, for the worship of Ba'al was being carried on under the name of Yahweh. The "Religious Right" uses the name of Jesus to cover the absolute claims of one national tradition. (See 1 Kings 13; and see Karl Barth's

extended commentary thereon in *Church Dogmatics* II /
2, 393ff.)

But the rhetoric of the "Moral Majority" is only a
further development of the ideologizing of politics that
stems from the Enlightenment. Ghita Ionescu, in *Politics
and the Pursuit of Happiness,* has traced the story from
what he calls the "Jacobin proto-system of political happiness" through its liberal-utilitarian and Marxist developments to the situation we are in now. Politics, as Ionescu
understands it, is "the regulation of the coexistence of
human beings within a unit of rule, with a view to im-
proving it in the present and in the future."[14] The Enlightenment gave birth to a new conception of politics, namely,
that happiness can be provided by a political system and
that the goal of politics is happiness.

The project of bringing heaven down to earth always
results in bringing hell up from below. The full revelation
of the heavenly city lies beyond the horizon of earthly
history. But the vision of it must control Christian action
within history, and such action can admit no separation
of private from public life. While the church can never
identify itself with the kingdom and must seek only the
role of a servant, witness, and sign of the kingdom, yet the
church can never admit any limitations of its role to the
private sector. The church witnesses to that true end for
which all creation and all human beings exist, the truth by
which all alleged values are to be judged. And truth must
be public truth, truth for all. A private truth for a limited
circle of believers is no truth at all. Even the most devout
faith will sooner or later falter and fail unless those who
hold it are willing to bring it into public debate and to test
it against experience in every area of life. If the Christian
faith about the source and goal of human life is to be
denied access to the public realm, where decisions are
made on the great issues of the common life, then it cannot in the long run survive even as an option for a minority.

If, as I believe, there can neither be a total identification
of the church and political order, nor a total separation

---

14. G. Ionescu, *Politics and the Pursuit of Happiness,* pp. 1-2.

between them, then there is room for much discussion of the ways in which their relationship is to be ordered. The question of how the Christian witness is to influence the public life in a post-Enlightenment society will occupy us in the final chapter. Before closing this one, however, let me try to suggest something of what the content of the vision should be. Both capitalism and socialism draw strength from a vision of human life, and this vision sustains them in face of their failures. For capitalism it is the vision of freedom—the freedom of the individual person to develop his own powers, to achieve the greatest success he is capable of and to enjoy the fruit of his achievement. For socialism it is the vision of equality; at its best this has been a vision of brotherhood, of community, but in practice it has often been reduced to the vision of a mere equality of rights for each person seen as an autonomous individual. In the one case, freedom is pursued at the cost of equality; in the other, equality is pursued at the cost of freedom. Both derive from the Enlightenment vision of human beings as autonomous individuals with innate and equal rights to pursue self-chosen ends to the limit of their powers. Each ideology can accuse the other of violating a faith they both hold by the denial of freedom on one side and by the denial of equality on the other.

I believe that the Christian view of God's purpose for the human family is different from both of these and arises from a distinct belief about what human nature is. From its first page to its last, the Bible is informed by a vision of human nature for which neither freedom nor equality is fundamental; what is fundamental is relatedness. Man—male and female—is made for God in such a way that being in the image of God involves being bound together in this most profound of all mutual relations. God binds himself in a covenant relationship with men and women to which he remains faithful at whatever cost and however unfaithful his covenant partner is. And people and nations are called to live in binding covenant relationships of brotherhood. Human beings reach their true end in such relatedness, in bonds of mutual love and obedience that reflect the mutual relatedness in love that is the being of the Triune God himself. Neither *freedom* nor *equality* are words that can take us to the heart of the matter. The breakdown of relationships will destroy freedom and will destroy equality, but neither of these will be achieved by being sought for itself. True freedom is not found by seeking to develop the powers of the self without limit, for the human person is not made for autonomy but for true relatedness in love and obedience; and this also entails the acceptance of limits as a necessary part of what it means to be human. Nor will the quest for equality create real justice, for justice—the giving to each of what is proper—can only be realized in a mutual relatedness in which each gives to the other the love and obedience that enable all to be truly human. Apart from this, the quest for justice becomes self-destructive, since it is of the very essence of fallen human nature that each of us overestimates what is due to the self and underestimates what is due to the other.

The fact that the argument between the political right and left—the argument between freedom and equality—has become as intellectually futile as it is practically lethal is illustrated on a small scale by the contemporary debate in Britain and elsewhere about the viability of the welfare state. The welfare state is an attempt to achieve a synthesis, or at least a balance, between freedom and equality. It accepts the operation of the free market, but it attempts to lessen the resulting inequalities through government action. It is attacked from the right by those who say that the cost of welfare provision for the disadvantaged is crushing the economic infrastructure. It is attacked from the left by those who say that the inequalities created by the free market are too great to be rectified by present welfare policies. Both sides accept and use the language of rights—the right to freedom on the one hand, and the right to a reasonably equitable share of resources on the other.

The argument of the left assumes that *need* creates a right that has priority over the *wants* of those who wish to pursue personal happiness in the way they choose. Two difficulties immediately appear: 1) Needs can be accorded priority over wants only if there is some socially accepted view of the goal of human existence. My wants may be (and often are) irrational; I can (and often do) want things that would not in the end bring me lasting happiness. My real needs, what I need to reach my true end, may be different from the wants I feel. But there cannot be a socially accepted priority for needs over wants unless there is a socially accepted doctrine of what human needs really are, in other words, a socially accepted doctrine of the nature and destiny of the human being. Such a socially accepted doctrine is excluded by the dogma of pluralism that controls post-Enlightenment society. 2) In the absence of a socially accepted doctrine of human destiny, how can needs be assessed? Students of the problem of poverty in affluent societies generally agree that poverty has to be defined in relation to the standard of living of society as a whole. A family in the deprived area of an English city may be wealthy in comparison with a family in a Bangladesh village, but if it is deprived of the things most British people enjoy, it is poor. The "poverty line" in an affluent society thus rises as the well-to-do find more and more ways of satisfying their wants. This leaves us with our initial problem unmet. If the needs of the poor are measured by the wants of the rich, we are left without a basis for determining which needs have priority over which wants.

Defenders of the welfare state seek to meet these difficulties by pointing to basic needs that must be met whatever our view of human nature and destiny may be, needs that must hence in all circumstances be accorded priority over wants. Professor Raymond Plant and his colleagues define these basic needs as "survival and autonomy."[15] This is clearly a rephrasing of the classic "life and liberty." One must agree that these needs are basic and must be met if any other needs or wants are to be considered, but this definition reduces human need to the merely biological level. And that is what must happen if equality is taken as the governing principle for life in society. We are all

15. See Plant, Lesser, and Taylor-Gooby, *Political Philosophy and Social Welfare,* pp. 38ff.

equal in our basic need for survival; this is the need we share with the animals. But to be human means to need other things—respect, honor, love. These needs, social rather than merely biological, call precisely for differentiation rather than for equality. Respect, honor, love—these terms have meaning only in the specific contexts in which they denote the particular kinds of respect, honor, and love one owes teachers, colleagues, parents, friends, wife, husband, children. It is this kind of differentiated respect, honor, and love that makes life human. An undifferentiated acknowledgment of the basic biological needs of a human being does not. And these things—respect, honor, and love—can not be claimed as rights. The descent of King Lear from the position of king and father to that of a "poor forked animal" in the wild heath began when he claimed the love of his daughters as a right.[16] It is only within a shared community of mutual respect, honor, and love freely given that needs are acknowledged as the ground for claims of right. To affirm the abstract and undifferentiated right of every autonomous individual to life, liberty, and the pursuit of happiness does not lead to a humane society.

But the counterarguments of the right are equally unsustainable. The myth of the "invisible band" that ensures that the untrammeled exercise of covetousness by each individual will produce the happiness of all is surely one of the most malignant falsehoods that has ever deceived the human race. It is a matter of history that, since the rise of capitalism, no freely elected government has been able to stand aside and leave society to the working of the forces of the free market. The obscene cruelties of the early phases of the Industrial Revolution in Britain under the ideology of capitalism compelled governments at an early stage to intervene for the protection of the victims. This is because no society can cohere and no government can continue to govern indefinitely when the exploitation of the weak by the strong passes a certain point and the political order has lost its moral credibility.

16. See the profound study *The Needs of Strangers* (1984) by Michael Ignatieff, pp. 27-53.

The contemporary attempts of the governments of Prime Minister Thatcher in Britain and of President Reagan in the United States can only destroy our societies.

But they will not be prevented from doing so by ideologies that rest on the same mythological beliefs about the equal right of every autonomous individual to life, liberty, and the pursuit of happiness. Falsehood can be overcome only by the truth, and the truth has been manifested once for all in Jesus Christ. It is the business of the church to bear witness in the public realm to that truth.

Human beings find fulfillment not in the attempt to develop themselves, not in the effort to better their own condition, not in the untrammeled exercise of unlimited covetousness, but in the experience of mutual relatedness and responsibility in serving a shared goal. Recent surveys in Britain have brought out the fact that great numbers of people have affirmed that the best years of their lives were those in which they shared the experience of the war. The bombing of cities, the destruction of homes, the absence of rest or holiday, the shortage of food and clothing, and the constant presence of death were all part of the picture; but what colors it all is the memory of shared commitment to a common purpose. That is what brings human beings to their very best, and most of us know it. Part of the terrible irony of war is that it enlists the best in human nature for purposes of mutual destruction. But to eliminate from the public life of a nation any accepted vision of a shared goal, leaving each individual to pursue self-chosen goals and making covetousness the prime mover of human affairs, is to invite destruction in another way, destruction from within. Who can deny that we are witnessing this destruction in the affluent societies of today?

War may provide for a time the sense of shared commitment and responsibility, but it is at the cost of dismembering the human family as a whole. What accepted vision can there be that can transcend the conflicting purposes of nations, classes, and races and draw all humankind into mutual responsibility? There have never been lacking candidates for this place. World history is

full of the dreams of a new order that will draw all humankind together. When these dreams are ours, we call them
dreams of world brotherhood; when others try to make
their dreams come true, we call it imperialism. Imperialism is the name we give to other people's proposals for
human unity. And, of course, we are right: every proposal
for human unity that does not specify the center around
which that unity is to be created, necessarily has the will,
the vision, the beliefs of the proposer as its implied center.
There can be no center for the unity of the human race
except in him who said, "I, when I am lifted up from the
earth, will draw all men to myself" (John 12:32). For the
Cross of Christ is the place of expiation, a place where sin
is forgiven; and the claim of the sinful self to make itself
and its dream the center of the world is set aside in favor
of the one whose claim alone is valid. Here is the one and
only center that has been given for the unity of humankind and thus the one object that can bind nations into
unity without setting them at enmity with one another.
The church as a truly universal supranational society is
the bearer of the vision that alone can give to each nation
a true unity of purpose. But if it is to do that, it must
accept in every nation the responsibility of placing all
public life — political, economic, and cultural — in the light
of its gospel. It must affirm that the central shrine of a
nation's life cannot remain empty, that if Christ is not
there then an idol will certainly take his place. How the
church is to fulfill this responsibility is the subject of my
final chapter. That it must do so is, I believe, a necessity
that arises from the very heart of the gospel.

6. What must we be? The Call to the Church

The church is the bearer to all the nations of a gospel that announces the kingdom, the reign, and the sovereignty of God. It calls men and women to repent of their false loyalty to other powers, to become believers in the one true sovereignty, and so to become corporately a sign, instrument, and foretaste of that sovereignty of the one true and living God over all nature, all nations, and all human lives. It is not meant to call men and women out of the world into a safe religious enclave but to call them out in order to send them back as agents of God's kingship. What does the calling imply for a church faced with the tough, powerful, and all-penetrating culture that we have been considering in these chapters?

It cannot imply a renewal of the attempt to create the kind of synthesis of church and state that shaped the life of western Europe for a thousand years. We can and must acknowledge our incalculable debt to the medieval church, which created a reasonably just and stable order out of the chaos of northern European barbarism and gave birth to the world that we have inherited—its science, its political democracy, and its traditions of ethical behavior. But there is no way in which we can, and no sense in which we should, attempt to reestablish the medieval *corpus Christianum.*

Nor, on the other hand, can we accept the view that the only task of the church is to provide for individuals a place in the private sector where they can enjoy an inward religious security but are not required to challenge the ideology that rules the public life of nations. The privilege of the Christian life cannot be sought apart from its responsibilities. The Christ who said, "Come unto me and I will give you rest," also said to those same disciples, "As the Father sent me so I send you," and showed them the scars of his battle with the rulers of the world (John 20:20-21).

But if we reject both of these proposals, there is still a wide field in which it is difficult to find our way. How is the Christian responsibility to proclaim and embody the kingship of God over the life of nations to be exercised in practice? If I am not mistaken, the predominant note in

the contemporary answers to this question is the note of
protest. The political order, with its entrenched interests
and its use of coercion to secure them, is identified as the
enemy, the primary locus of evil. The place of the church
is thus not in the seats of the establishment but in the
camps and marching columns of the protesters. The protest may be pacifist, claiming in the name of Christ to
renounce all coercion; or it may be political and revolutionary, claiming to embody an alternative order of government. In either case, the protesters contend that as
Jesus was crucified outside the wall of the city, so the place
of the Christian must always be outside the citadel of the
establishment and on the side of its victims. Only from
this position, they claim, will things be seen as they truly
are. Attempts of the kind that were often made earlier in
this century—to bring together Christians in responsible
positions in government, industry, and commerce to discuss the bearing of their faith on their daily practice—they
dismiss as elitist and therefore incapable of generating
true insights. A person who wields power cannot see truth;
that is the privilege of the powerless.

It is easy to point out that the popularity of this kind
of view owes something to the Marxist idea of the proletariat as the messianic people, history's bearer of the promise of truth and life. But to acknowledge that does not
silence the argument. Jesus was indeed crucified by the
established powers. Does it not follow that to go with
Jesus on the way of the Cross must mean to be on the side
of those who suffer from the powers of the established
order and not of those who wield these powers? Can one
who goes the way of the Cross sit in the seat of Pilate when
it falls vacant? I do not find it easy to answer this question,
and yet it cannot be evaded. Certainly, a church that sees
the cross of Jesus as the central event of history can never
identify any political order with the reign of God. There
cannot be what Islam has set out to establish: a single
Sharia, which controls a single society in all its life—
political and religious. It is only possible to entertain that
idea if one denies the biblical account of the radical sinfulness of human nature, a sinfulness that no social order

will remove. If the Cross is the place where the reality of human nature is unmasked, then the idea of a perfect earthly society is an illusion. There cannot be such. But, equally certainly, the Cross must be interpreted in its true context, in the biblical narrative taken as a whole and in the context of a fully Trinitarian doctrine of God.

We misunderstand Jesus and his death if we see him simply as the greatest of those who have died in revolt against established power. Jesus died as the beloved Son of the Father, by whom the powers that killed him are authorized. It was the almighty Father who delivered up his Son to death for our sake. During his trial, Jesus acknowledged the fact that Pilate's authority to deliver him to death was given to him by God (John 19:11); what he condemned was the abuse of this authority. Kingship in the human sense—the authority to rule over a people—is, according to Scripture, something authorized by God and also something constantly corrupted by human sin. This is brought out with exemplary clarity in the accounts of the establishment of the kingship in 1 Samuel 8 and 9. Jesus did not set out to destroy the rule exercised by the Roman and Jewish establishment. By manifesting and exercising the true kingship of God, he exposed their corruption and thereby, as Paul says, disarmed them, robbed them of their pretensions to absolute authority. He exercised his kingship by bearing witness to the truth—to the one great reality against which all claims to reality have to be tested (John 18:37). All kingship from Calvary onward is tested and judged by the standard of the true kingship established there; judged and tested, not eliminated. The powers were disarmed, but they were not destroyed. According to the Pauline teaching, the principalities and powers, which can become the agents of evil, and which were unmasked and robbed of their pretensions to absolute authority when they put Jesus on the cross, are nevertheless created in Christ and for Christ and still continue to function after Christ's decisive victory, yet only under his authority (Col. 2:15; 1:15-16; 1 Cor. 2:6-8).

To unpack these Pauline ideas, let us return to the gospel narrative. The first commentary on the death of

Jesus was the suicide of Judas. If the cross were the last word in God's self-revelation, then this first commentary would be the only possible one. If all humankind—even in its best representatives—is exposed here as one murderous treason against its Creator, what future is there but death? What is the point of continuing this futile saga of sin, even with all the adornments of civilization? If the cross is the end, then there is no future.

But it is not. The resurrection is the revelation to chosen witnesses of the fact that Jesus who died on the cross is indeed king—conqueror of death and sin, Lord and Savior of all. The resurrection is not the reversal of a defeat but the proclamation of a victory. The King reigns from the tree. The reign of God has indeed come upon us, and its sign is not a golden throne but a wooden cross.

But what does that mean in practice? In what sense that has any practical consequences can we say these things? Can powerlessness wield power? Must not the crucifixion of the king mean the end of every kind of kingship that collaborated in his crucifixion? Surely now all traditional embodiments of kingship, of political rule, stand exposed and condemned before the kingship that is exercised in the cross. Surely now is the moment for the kingship of God to appear, displacing all other forms of sovereignty. That is the natural and obvious inference, it would seem, that must be drawn and that the disciples do draw once they have become convinced that the death of Jesus is not the end of his claim to kingship: "Lord, will you now restore the kingdom to Israel?" (Acts 1:6). It is the obvious question. Jesus' answer is a warning and a promise that together define the role of the church with respect to the kingdom *post Christum*. It is first a warning: God alone is king, and he retains in his own authority the decision on when and how to manifest his kingship. "It is not for you to know times or seasons which the Father has fixed by his own authority" (Acts 1:7). We are required to bide the Father's time. We do not establish his kingdom; it is, quite simply, his rule.

But there is also a promise: it is the promise of the Spirit whose presence is the pledge and foretaste of the kingdom and becomes for the church a witness to that kingship vis-à-vis the continuing powers of this age (Acts 1:8). The continuing existence of these powers, sustaining an order—albeit with much distortion and corruption—in which some measure of justice and freedom are secured, is a work of God, who in his mercy gives a time and a space for men and women to recognize the true kingship, to repent, and to believe. These powers are ordained by God and are to be respected. They are appointed, as Paul says, to punish the wrongdoer and to reward those who do well. Thus the Christian is not to seek justice for himself by taking the law into his own hands, for there is one appointed by God to establish justice, a servant of God for your good, as Paul says (Rom. 12:17–13:4). Consequently, Paul himself does not hesitate to appeal to the established authorities for justice in his own case (e.g., Acts 25:10-11).

The Christian, therefore, has no right to be indifferent to the good working of those authorities which God has ordained for a good purpose but which can easily become instruments of wickedness. We know that it is God's kingship alone that has the last word, and we are witnesses of that kingship through the presence and power of the Holy Spirit, who is God's kingly power in liberating and sanctifying action. That kingly power is at work in the preaching, healing, and serving witness of the church to call men and women to their true allegiance. But a true allegiance can only be given in freedom, and it is the gracious will of the Father, whose patience is great beyond our reckoning, to provide a space and a time within the present order wherein that allegiance can be freely given—or withheld. We have no right to try to foreclose on God's patience and, in the name of God's kingship, to disown responsibility for the forms of earthly rule—sinful as they are—that God provides for the maintenance of such a measure of order and freedom as is possible for sinful human beings. When the classical world-view and the Roman imperial power, which had seemed invincible and eternal in the first century of our era, disintegrated and lost their power to rule, Christians would have been wrong to refuse responsibility for the exercise of political power. Rulers, like all human beings, can act with vigor and patience only in the power of some sustaining vision of how things really are—of the order, the *dharma,* the *Tao* that governs all things. When the classical vision faded and the pagan empire disintegrated, it was right that those who had been given a new vision of the eternal order through the Incarnation of the Son of God should accept the responsibility of seeking to shape public life in the power of that vision. The attempt to create a Christian civilization, to shape laws consonant with the biblical teaching, to place kings and emperors under the explicit obligation of Christian discipleship—none of this was wrong. On the contrary, to have declined these immense responsibilities would have been an act of apostasy. It would have been an abandonment of the faith of the gospel.

By the same token, the church today cannot without guilt absolve itself from the responsibility, where it sees the possibility, of seeking to shape the public life of nations and the global ordering of industry and commerce in the light of the Christian faith. Even where the church is a tiny minority with no political power, it has the duty to address the governing authority of the civil community with the word of God. This is what the brave churches of Taiwan and Korea, for example, are doing today; the church reminds them of the fact that—whether they know him or not—Christ is the judge before whom they must stand in the end to give account of their stewardship of the power he gave them. With that responsibility comes, necessarily, the duty of regular and public prayer for the governing authorities. Even when the church lives under a brutal tyranny, it still has the double duty and must discharge it fearlessly, as Archbishop Luwum of Uganda did when he confronted the dictator Amin with the word of God and paid for it with his life. And most certainly when the church enjoys freedom and influence, and when it includes a large part of the population in a democratically ordered society, it cannot be absolved from this responsibility. How this is to be done is the question with which we must wrestle; but that it must be done is certain.

Of course, the distinction of church and state has to be maintained and would have to be maintained even if every citizen of the state were also a member of the church. Church and state have different tasks, but both receive their mandate from the God who is revealed in Christ, and both are responsible to him. This is true whether governments acknowledge it or not. The necessary distinction between them with respect to their powers and responsibilities does not negate the fact that those who exercise political authority are responsible to God—the only God, Father, Son, and Holy Spirit—and it is the duty of the church to remind them in season and out of season of that fact. Whatever the form of government—monarchy, oligarchy, democracy, one-party rule, or any combination of these—there are in fact men and women who exercise power over their fellow men and women. Their authority to do so rests on God's gracious ordering of his world. They are sinful men and women who may and do misuse the power entrusted to them. But they are nonetheless responsible for both doing the right and acknowledging the truth; and the church always has the God-given responsibility, which it may not evade, of reminding them of that fact.

I am well aware that this doctrine is unacceptable in a society and at a time when the concept that the state is secular, in the sense of morally and religiously neutral, has become almost an axiom. And while I believe that the idea of the secular state needs to be examined afresh, I cannot fail to acknowledge its persuasiveness. If we cannot disown all that we have inherited from the thousand-year experience of the medieval *corpus Christianum*, neither can we deny our immense and enduring debt to those of the Enlightenment who challenged the medieval world-view with the slogan "dare to know." We are witnessing in parts of the world of Islam today a powerful movement that, rejecting modernity, seeks to restore the rule of the *Sharia* over all of life, public and private. We cannot desire a similar movement among Christians. Nor do modern attempts to create a Christian state, as in Franco's Spain and Salazar's Portugal, inspire any desire to emulate. Can there be such a thing as a Christian state or a Christian society, and ought we to seek it?

There was a period when thinkers like Jacques Maritain in France, Hermann Dooyeweerd in the Netherlands, T. S. Eliot in England, and John Baillie in Scotland were sketching their visions of a Christian society. They looked at the movements in Russia, Italy, and Germany that had succeeded in taking over the whole ordering of national life on the strength of an ideology passionately believed by a vigorous minority. They saw the corrupt and hopelessly lethargic democracies of Italy and Germany transformed into dynamic societies by the power of these ideologies. They asked themselves whether it could not be possible for Christians, as a dedicated group even if a minority, to do something comparable: to give the rudderless democracies a sense of direction and purpose, yet without the repression and intolerance that marked the totalitarian movements. It was a noble vision, and it was not without effect. In Britain one can certainly point to great changes that were made possible in considerable measure by the exercise of explicitly Christian conviction in the field of politics. But the 1960s saw a sharp swing in the opposite direction. Munby's book *The Idea of a Secular Society,* published in 1963, was a direct rebuttal of Eliot's *Idea of a Christian Society.* "Secularity" became the blessed word for theologians of the 1960s. The accepted vision was of a public world totally liberated from its tutelage by the church, and of a state that eschewed any religious or ideological commitments, holding the ring equally for all. This view regards Gladstone's position, to which I referred in the first chapter—that the state is a moral personality and therefore responsible to do the right and to acknowledge the truth—as a mere survival of medievalism.

But Gladstone was surely right when he pointed out that the Roman Empire could give equal tolerance to all religions just because it could be quite adamant about something much more important than religion, something required to keep society from disintegrating, namely, the veneration of the emperor. On that there could be no compromise, and I think we have to acknowledge at least some truth in Gladstone's argument. No state can be completely secular in the sense that those who exercise power have no beliefs about what is true and no commitments to what they believe to be right. It is the duty of the church to ask what those beliefs and commitments are and to expose them to the light of the gospel. There is no genuinely missionary encounter of the gospel with our culture unless this happens. Here we must face frankly the distortion of the gospel that is perpetrated in a great deal that passes for missionary encounter. A preaching of the gospel that calls men and women to accept Jesus as Savior but does not make it clear that discipleship means commitment to a vision of society radically different from that which controls our public life today must be condemned as false.

The South African missiologist David Bosch has pointed out how much damage has been done by the usual English translation of *dikaiosune* as "righteousness" and the consequent insulation of an idea of inward and spiritual righteousness from an outward and manifest justice in social relationships. Spanish-speaking Christians are less tempted to fall into this trap because the one word *justiia* is universally used to translate *dikaiosune.* It is easy to see how the use of the two different English words *righteous* and *just* for the single biblical word *dikaios,* and the consistent translation of *dikaiosune* in the New Testament as "righteousness" while the Hebrew equivalent *tsedeq* is translated both as "justice" and as "righteousness," has seduced evangelical Christians into a mental separation between righteousness as an inward and spiritual state and justice as an outward and political program. But to accept this dichotomy is to abandon the gospel and surrender to the pressure of our pagan culture. As we have seen over and over again in this study, this dichotomy between the private and the public worlds is the central clue to the ideology that governs our culture. To accept it is to make the surrender the early church refused to make—at the cost of the blood of countless martyrs.

A private religion of personal salvation that did not

challenge the public ideology was perfectly safe under Roman law, as it is safe under ours. On these terms the church of the first three centuries could have flourished under the rule of Caesar precisely as this kind of evangelicalism flourishes under the protection of our kind of society. But the authentic gospel cannot accept this kind of relegation. The sovereign rule of God requires that the state acknowledge its responsibility to reflect in all its ordering of society the justice of God—a justice that is primarily embodied in covenant relationships of mutual responsibility. To make disciples is to call and equip men and women to be signs and agents of God's justice in all human affairs. An evangelism that invites men and women to accept the name of Christ but fails to call them to this real encounter must be rejected as false.

But how is it to happen? How, in practice, is the church to challenge our culture in its public as well as its private aspects in the name of Christ? What kind of churchmanship will enable us so to preach the gospel that men and women are called to be disciples in the fullest sense—men and women and children whose personal and corporate life is a sign, instrument, and foretaste of God's kingly rule over all creation and all nations? How, in particular, are we to do this, we who are sent not to one of the ancient world religions but to a society nourished in its deepest roots by a Christian tradition but governed in its explicit assumptions by a pagan ideology? And how can we be missionaries to this modern world, we who are ourselves part of this modern world? As has often been remarked, we are at a point in history comparable to the one occupied by Augustine. He stood at the point where the classical vision had lost its power over people's minds, and society was disintegrating. He was the one who formulated for the Western half of Christendom a vision based on the twin dogmas of Trinity and Incarnation, which was to shape public life for a thousand years and to create a community in which the Christian life could be nourished. Alasdair MacIntyre, who invokes the memory of that moment to illuminate our situation, adds, however, that there is one great difference between Augustine's time and ours: then the barbarians were waiting outside the gates, but now they are already in the seats of power. And, says MacIntyre, "it is our lack of consciousness of this that constitutes our predicament."[1] If that is true, as I think it is, we must ask what the conditions are for the recovery by the church of its proper distinction from, and its proper responsibility for, this secular culture that we have shared so comfortably and so long with what MacIntyre would call the barbarians. I want to close by listing seven essentials for the answering of this question.

1. The first must be the recovery and firm grasp of a true doctrine of the last things, of eschatology. The gospel is good news of the kingdom, and the kingdom is an eschatological concept. A true understanding of the last things is the first essential.

We are very familiar with the way language about the kingdom of God has been used to domesticate Christianity within the post-Enlightenment world-view. The thinkers of the Enlightenment believed that the liberation of the human mind and conscience from the shackles of dogma would lead to the gradual elimination of ignorance and of evil and thus to the progress of humanity toward the heavenly city—a perfect commonwealth of free and happy people. The underlying ideas here are not biblical but classical. What is presupposed is an inherent power within history that leads toward perfection. The opposing power is not sin, not a radical distortion at the center of human reason and conscience, but just the inertia of nature. We are familiar with the way liberal Protestant Christianity used the biblical language of the kingdom to give a pious coloring to the dominant ideology. Seeking the kingdom meant working for social progress. We are also familiar with the way the Marxists—more biblical here than the liberal Protestants—gave an apocalyptic twist to the Enlightenment scenario and proclaimed the classless society only on the other side of the final Armageddon, in which the messianic proletariat will destroy the kingdom of evil. The problem with both these views is that they

---

1. A. MacIntyre, *After Virtue*, p. 245.

marginalize the human being. The men and women who now serve and fight for the new society will not see it themselves. In regard to the ultimate goal of history, they are expendable means, not ultimate ends. And so, inevitably, alongside the doctrine of progress there comes back the ancient pre-Christian idea of the immortality of the soul. The individual person finds the true end of his living and striving not in the perfect society, which only the remote posterity will see, but in an afterlife in another world, which has no relation to this. The two histories—my personal history and the history of the world—go their separate ways to different ends. My personal future and the future of the world have no essential relationship to each other. Human life is no longer a unity; it falls apart into two divisions: the private and the public, the spiritual and the political. We are back again at the dichotomy with which we have become so familiar in looking at our post-Enlightenment culture.

Yet the human person is a unity. I am the same person in my most private prayers and my most public acts. Whence comes the splitting apart of what we experience as a unity? It comes, of course, from the fact of death, the fact that at a point that is as unknown as it is certain I who pray and work must leave behind all my work, cut all those bonds that have from my birth bound me in one bundle of mutual responsibility with family, society, and world, and face alone the last horizon. This creates the split, tempting me to turn my back on the outward world of shared responsibilities and to find meaning exclusively in the pilgrimage of my own soul. Yet as a human being who still lives, I live not as a solitary individual but as one who depends for every day's living on a human world of shared responsibilities. I can only live as part of society, and I can only act in the light of some vision of the goal of the human journey as a whole. It is death that creates that fatal dichotomy between two worlds of meaning—one that sees ultimate meaning only in the destiny of my immortal soul and thus makes the public history of the world a story without meaning; the other that sees meaning only in the march of humanity toward a shared future, and thus makes the human person marginal and finally dispensable.

It is death that drives in this wedge and splits our vision of the future in two. And death is not, for human beings, merely a biological necessity; it is, as the Bible teaches us, the wages of sin—the outward and visible sign of an inward and spiritual fact, namely, that nothing in my life is fit for God's perfect kingdom. Because this is so, there can be no straight road from this life to the goal that alone gives it meaning. The gospel is good news at this point because Christ has overcome the power of sin and death. Entering completely into our shared humanity with all its burden of sin, he has gone down into the darkness of death and judgment for us, and, in his resurrection, given us a sign and foretaste of total victory. As united with him we are enabled to follow the same way. We do not see the future of either our own personal selves or the world we share with all people. The curtain of death shuts off our view. But Jesus has gone before us through the curtain. The road disappears from view down into a dark valley, into whose depth we cannot peer. Jesus has gone down there before us and has appeared victorious on the other side. He is himself the path, the way that goes through death to life (John 13:36–14:7). As we follow that way, we have before us, beyond the chasm of death, the vision of the holy city into which all the glory of the nations will be brought and from which everything unclean is excluded (Rev. 21, 22). Following that way, we can commit ourselves without reserve to all the secular work our shared humanity requires of us, knowing that nothing we do in itself is good enough to form part of that city's building, knowing that everything—from our most secret prayers to our most public political acts—is part of that sin-stained human nature that must go down into the valley of death and judgment, and yet knowing that as we offer it up to the Father in the name of Christ and in the power of the Spirit, it is safe with him and—purged in fire—it will find its place in the holy city at the end (cf. 1 Cor. 3:10-15).

This faith heals the split between the public and the private. There is no room for a political fanaticism that supposes that my political achievements will establish God's kingdom, or declares a holy war against opponents, or tramples on individual human beings in the pursuit of a political millennium. The public political act has its real meaning simply as a kind of acted prayer for the coming of God's reign. Equally, there is no room for a piety that seeks personal holiness by opting out of the struggle for a measure of justice and freedom in public life. This faith enables us to be politically realistic without cynicism, to be sensitive to the supreme rule of love without sentimentality. It enables us humbly to acknowledge that even the best social order is—in God's sight—an organization of sinful men and women and therefore always prone to corruption; and yet not to use this knowledge as an excuse for political quietism, but rather as an inspiration to work tirelessly for the best possible among the actually available political alternatives.

2. Second on my list of essentials for the quest of a Christian social order I will put a Christian doctrine of freedom. Surely the greatest gift the Enlightenment has left us is the recognition of the right of all people to freedom of thought and of conscience. It is a gift we can never surrender. And we have penitently to acknowledge that it was won in the teeth of determined opposition from the churches. We have to confess also, if we are to be honest, that the same churches that demanded freedom of conscience when they were in a minority have, when they became majorities, denied to others the freedom they claimed for themselves. How, if we are to think of a Christian society, can we ensure that the same sins are not repeated when and if Christians are in a position to impose their views on others? If we insist, as I have done, that the state has an obligation to recognize truth, how can the same state offer protection to something it recognizes as error? If there were a Christian state, would it not necessarily be intolerant? These are real questions to be faced.

We must begin by distinguishing toleration from neutrality or indifference. The latter was well described by

Gibbon when he said that in Roman society all religions were to the people equally true, to the philosophers equally false, and to the government equally useful. It would be difficult to deny that this is true of some of today's "developed" societies. But that kind of neutrality is evidence either of impending collapse or else of the fact that some other ideology has taken the place usually occupied by religion as the overarching "plausibility structure" for intellectual and political life. Since total skepticism about ultimate beliefs is strictly impossible, in that no belief can be doubted except on the basis of some other belief, indifference is always in danger of giving place to some sort of fanaticism that can be as intolerant as any religion has ever been. Tolerance with respect to what is not important is easy. How is it possible to combine real commitment to the truth in matters of supreme importance with tolerance of falsehood?

Clearly, if we are to be consistent, the answer has to be given from within our commitment to the truth as it is in Jesus and not sought from outside that truth. It can, I think, be given in the form of three statements. a) First, as we have seen earlier, the risen Jesus whose kingship was defined as bearing witness to the truth, warned the church against the temptation to expect immediately the manifestation of the truth in coercive power. It is the will of the Father to provide a space and a time wherein men and women can give their allegiance to the kingdom in the only way it can be given—namely, in freedom. To use the God-given authority of the state to deny that freedom is thus to violate the space God himself has provided and put into the care of earthly governors. b) Second, the church, which is entrusted with the truth, is a body of sinful men and women who falsely identify their grasp of truth with the truth itself. The paradox of grace, that the church is a body of forgiven sinners, both forgiven and sinful, applies to the church's understanding of the truth. At the very point of his confession of the truth, Peter could become an agent of Satan (Mark 8:29, 33). He grasped the truth but immediately made it an instrument of falsehood. Because sin remains a reality in the life of the forgiven community, the church can and does allow the truth entrusted to her to be turned into an ideological justification of her own human interests, and God constantly has to use his other servants, and especially the state, to bring the church to repentance.

c) This leads to the third statement, for which I turn to the Johannine discourses, in which our Lord is represented as telling his disciples that they still have much to learn of the truth that cannot be told them immediately, and that the Spirit who will be given to them will lead them into all the truth. The context of these sayings is the long account of the missionary experience that lies ahead of the church, its rejection by the world, and the witness the Spirit will give in speaking for the church, in confuting the wisdom of the world, and in glorifying Jesus by taking all that belongs to the Father and showing it to the church as the possession of the Son (John 15:18–16:15). This promise is being fulfilled as the church goes on its missionary journey to the ends of the earth and the end of time, entering into dialogue with new cultures and being itself changed as new things that are part of the Father's world are brought through the Spirit into Christ's treasury. In this missionary dialogue the church both learns new things and provides the place where witness is borne to Christ as head of the human race, and where he is seen more and more for what he is, as new tongues confess him as Lord.

Thus a true understanding of the gospel itself ought to enable Christians to be firm in their allegiance to Christ as the way, the truth, and the life, and also to be ready to enter into a genuinely listening dialogue with those who do not give this allegiance but from whom they know that they have to be ready to learn. The mind that is firmly anchored in Christ—knowing that Christ is much greater than the limited understanding of him each of us has—is at the same time able to enter freely into the kind of missionary dialogue I have described. This is the foundation on which a true tolerance, not indifference to the truth, can be founded. True dialogue is as far as possible from neutrality or indifference. Its basis is the shared conviction that there is truth to be known and that we must both bear witness to the truth given to us and also listen to the witness of others.

With such an understanding, we can envision a state (whether or not such a thing is a present political possibility) that acknowledges the Christian faith as true, but deliberately provides full security for those of other views. It would be different from both the Christian states of the past that suppressed dissenting minorities and from the pluralistic states of the present that profess to be guided by no vision of human nature and destiny—but are in fact guided by a very specific ideology, namely, the ideology of the Enlightenment (as, for example, Muslim minorities in Britain are very acutely aware). It would be a state embodying the idea of the proper role of the political order that the Bible seems to suggest.

I suppose that the crucial test of such an idea would lie in its implications for education. There is no area where the issues are more immediate and more difficult than this. Whatever we may say about the religious neutrality of the state, the experience of passing through school and university is shaping the minds of young people in certain directions. It is not and cannot be religiously neutral. The omission of religion from the curriculum is itself a momentous statement about what society believes and expects its children to believe. And when we have, as in Britain today, a Muslim community that constitutes 6 percent of the population and over 80 percent in some of the inner-city schools, we discover that the very idea of treating religion as a subject that can be put into a list alongside physics, history, and literature is itself an assault on the foundations of belief. There are no answers to the questions raised here unless one accepts that human societies have to live through the experience of real conflict between ultimate truth claims. Any idea that one can be neutral is an illusion. I believe that the Christian gospel provides and opens up the possibility of a life—public and personal—that includes both the ability to hold vital convictions that lead to action and also the capacity to preserve for others the freedom to dissent.

The relationship of the Christian understanding of freedom to that which has provided the central thrust of the Enlightenment must necessarily be a critical one. Seen from a biblical perspective, a human being is not and can never be autonomous. Consequently, liberation in the Bible is always seen as a change of regime, or jurisdiction, from the false dominion to the true, from serving Pharaoh to serving Yahweh (Exod. 3:13; 6:6), from serving sin and death to serving God (Rom. 6:20-23). From the point of view of the Enlightenment, the biblical idea of freedom is paradoxical—a freedom of the one who serves the true master. From the point of view of the Bible, the freedom celebrated in the Enlightenment is the freedom offered by the serpent in Eden, the freedom to make one's own decision about what is good. By accepting that offer, we put ourselves under the domination of powers that lead to destruction. We become, as Paul says, the slaves of sin. True freedom is a gift of grace given by the one who is in fact Lord; that gift, freely given, can only be received in freedom. It follows that the church cannot bear witness to that gift unless there is freedom to refuse it. Yet the church must still bear witness that this is the only true freedom: to belong wholly to the one by whom the space of freedom is created, and whose service is perfect freedom.

3. As the third requirement for a missionary encounter with our culture, I would list what might be called a "de-clericalized" theology. I can perhaps indicate what I mean by referring to a moving passage in Teilhard de Chardin's little classic of the spiritual life, *Le Milieu Divin.* He is speaking of the challenge put to the Christian who is also a scientist by his non-Christian colleague. The latter says something like the following: "We who take our science seriously cannot completely trust you who are a Christian. For, however brilliant your scientific work may be, we know that you are not ultimately serious about it. For you, the ultimately serious matters are in a world beyond science. For you, science is not ultimately important. In the last judgment, as you conceive it, it will not matter whether your conclusions were right or wrong: the only questions asked will be about your sincerity, your devotion to truth, your humility, etc. Really, your science is only a kind of game, a playground in which you can exercise your spiritual muscles. You are not really serious."[2]

Teilhard acknowledges the force of this. Traditional Christian teaching has been otherworldly in its emphasis. It has had more to say about how to accept failure than about how to succeed, more about suffering than about action. Theology has been the preserve of those who minister as priests and pastors to the inner spiritual life of their people. Consequently, when theologians whose whole work is in this pastoral ministry try to speak about matters of politics and economics, their words do not carry weight. And Christian men and women who are deeply involved in secular affairs view theology as the arcane pursuit of professional clergymen. This withdrawal of theology from the world of secular affairs is made more complete by the work of biblical scholars whose endlessly fascinating exercises have made it appear to the lay Christian that no one untrained in their methods can really understand anything the Bible says. We are in a situation analogous to one about which the great Reformers complained. The Bible has been taken out of the hands of the layperson; it has now become the professional property not of the priesthood but of the scholars. Since the demise of the biblical theology movement, few Christians dare to appeal to the authority of Scripture in making a political decision.

The missionary encounter with our culture for which I am pleading will require the energetic fostering of a declericalized, lay theology. Of course, I am not asking for something previously unheard of. Forty years ago Hendrik Kraemer, W. A. Visser 't Hooft, and Suzanne de Dietrich had this vision and embodied it in the Ecumenical Institute at Bossey, where in the succeeding years a stream of laypeople from all over the world have caught a glimpse of it. But this is a small ship to carry a cargo for the whole worldwide church. We need a multitude of places where this kind of lay theology can be nourished. We need much

---

2. Teilhard de Chardin, *Le Milieu Divin*, p. 68.

better provision to ensure that when church leaders make pronouncements on ethical, political, and economic questions, their words are informed by a theology that has been wrought out at the coal face, at the place where faith wrestles at personal cost with the hard issues of public life. And we need to create, above all, possibilities in every congregation for laypeople to share with one another the actual experience of their weekday work and to seek illumination from the gospel for their daily secular duty. Only thus shall we begin to bring together what our culture has divided—the private and the public. Only thus will the church fulfill its proper missionary role. For while there are occasions when it is proper for the church, through its synods and hierarchies, to make pronouncements on public issues, it is much more important that all its lay members be prepared and equipped to think out the relationship of their faith to their secular work. Here is where the real missionary encounter takes place.

There is an area here that has been worked over by Dutch theologians but little noticed (as far as I know) by Anglo-Saxon theology. I am thinking of the work of Abraham Kuyper and Hermann Dooyeweerd on what the former called "sphere sovereignty" (*souvereiniteit in eigen kring*), namely, the doctrine that God had given—as part of the order of creation—a measure of autonomy to each of the major areas of human life, including such areas as art, science, politics, ethics, and faith. This means that the human community that is responsible for the development of each of these spheres is responsible directly to God and not to the community of faith (the church), which has no direct authority over them. "Sphere sovereignty implies that each sphere in society has a God-given task and competence which are limited by the sphere's own intrinsic nature."[3] Dooyeweerd's development of this idea is, in my view, too scholastic and inadequately related to biblical authority, but it seems to me an important line of thinking that avoids both the post-Enlightenment idea of the total autonomy of these spheres and the medieval idea that all these spheres should be under the authori-

---

3. H. Dooyeweerd, *Roots of Western Culture*, p. 22.

ty of the church. However, this line of thinking will be fruitful only if the work of scientists, economists, political philosophers, artists, and others is illuminated by insights derived from rigorous theological thinking. For such a declericalized theology, the role of the church will be that of servant, not mistress.

4. The fourth item in this suggested list of requirements for a missionary encounter with our culture is a radical theological critique of the theory and practice of denominationalism. Richard Niebuhr's dictum, "Denominationalism represents the moral failure of Christianity" has often been quoted; but he wrote that more than fifty-five years ago. Today the defense of denominationalism has become respectable. In a famous essay entitled "*Denominationalism as a Basis for Ecumenicity*" (1955), Winthrop Hudson defined and defended denominationalism in the following affirmations: no denomination claims to represent the whole church of Christ; none claims that all other churches are false churches; none claims that all members of society should be incorporated in its membership, none claims that society and the state should submit to its ecclesiastical regulation; but all recognize their shared responsibility for society. Negatively, therefore, a denomination is not a sect. Positively, to quote Sidney Mead, a denomination is "a voluntary association of like-hearted and like-minded individuals, who are united on the basis of common beliefs for the purpose of accomplishing tangible and defined objectives." One of the primary objectives is the propagation of its point of view.[4] It is a matter of historical fact that denominationalism as it flourishes in the United States today developed out of the voluntary associations that were formed for missionary purposes. In the essays from which I have quoted, the denomination is celebrated as the great gift of North American Christianity to the universal church. In the words of Karl Hertz, "Denominationalism is the new American way in Christianity."[5] And in a large part of the

4. Russell E. Richey, ed., *Denominationalism,* p. 167.
5. Ibid., p. 264.

world the denomination is seen as the natural form of the church.

Surely no one can deny that denominations have been and are powerful, purposeful, and effective agencies of self-propagation. The question that has to be asked is this: How serious is it that the denominational principle requires (as all its defenders agree) the surrender of any claim to be the church in the sense in which that word is used in the New Testament? It is clear that in the Pauline letters the name *Ecclesia tou Theou* is applied to actual visible bodies of sinful men and women defined simply by the names of the places where they lived—God's congregation in Corinth, Philippi, or Thessalonica. It is also applied to the whole body of such people in all places, since it is the same God who is assembling them in each place. These assemblies are the church. The exponents of the denominational principle acknowledge that a denomination does not and cannot claim to be *a* church or *the* church in any biblical sense. In their view, the church in its true being is invisible: the denomination is a partial manifestation of the church but makes no claim to be *the* church. It is a voluntary association based on the free personal choice of a number of individuals to cooperate for certain purposes, purposes that in the nineteenth century, when the great development of denominations took place, were described as the advancement of the kingdom.

It is the common observation of sociologists of religion that denominationalism is the religious aspect of secularization. It is the form that religion takes in a culture controlled by the ideology of the Enlightenment. It is the social form in which the privatization of religion is expressed. As Thomas Luckman says, "Once religion is defined as a private affair the individual may choose from the assortment of ultimate meanings as he sees fit."[6] The denomination provides a shelter for those who have made the same choice. It is thus in principle unable to confront the state and society as a whole with the claim with which Jesus confronted Pilate—the claim of the truth. It is not, in any biblical sense, the church.

It follows that neither a denomination separately nor

---

6. T. Luckman, *The Invisible Religion,* p. 99.

all the denominations linked together in some kind of federal unity or "reconciled diversity" can be the agents of a missionary confrontation with our culture, for the simple reason that they are themselves the outward and visible signs of an inward and spiritual surrender to the ideology of our culture. They cannot confront our culture with the witness of the truth since even for themselves they do not claim to be more than associations of individuals who share the same private opinions. A genuinely ecumenical movement, that is to say, a movement seeking to witness to the lordship of Christ over the whole inhabited *oikoumene* cannot take the form of a federation of denominations. It must patiently seek again what the Reformers sought—"to restore the face of the Catholic Church." One of the encouraging features of church life in England today is the growing number of "local ecumenical projects" that bring together the denominationally separated churches in one place in order to create a more coherent and credible Christian witness to the whole human community in that place. These are scattered, fragile, and vulnerable enterprises, but they indicate the direction in which the church must go.

5. As the fifth condition for a missionary encounter with our culture, I would list the necessity for help in seeing our own culture through Christian minds shaped by other cultures. Paul says that we need all the saints to comprehend the greatness of Christ (Eph. 3:14ff.). We need the witness of the whole ecumenical family if we are to be authentic witnesses of Christ to our own culture. I referred in an earlier chapter to the impression we receive when we look at the portraits of Jesus painted in different cultures. They make vividly clear how much our vision of Jesus is shaped by our culture. It cannot be otherwise. The fact that Jesus is much more than, much greater than our culture-bound vision of him can only come home to us through the witness of those who see him with other eyes. Asian and African Christians who received the gospel from European and American missionaries and therefore were invited to see Jesus as our culture saw him now struggle through their own study of Scripture and their own obedience in their own time and place to articulate a form of Christian believing and behaving in terms of their own cultures. We need their witness to correct ours, as indeed they need ours to correct theirs. At this moment our need is greater, for they have been far more aware of the dangers of syncretism, of an illegitimate alliance with false elements in their culture, than we have been. But whether it is we or they, we imperatively need one another if we are to be the faithful witnesses of Christ in our many different cultures.

For this reason the churches in the Western world must recognize that they cannot do without the World Council of Churches. When that Council held its second Assembly in Evanston in 1954, it was a great media event. There was immense enthusiasm throughout the nation, and even the secular press and radio were full of it. Today the World Council of Churches is widely regarded with deep suspicion in many parts of the Western world. The reason is obvious.

Thirty years ago the ecumenical movement was perceived as the worldwide triumph of our kind of Christianity. The colored and colorful representatives of the Asian and African churches were hailed and photographed as trophies of our missionary success. Today the ecumenical movement is perceived as a threat, and the theologies coming out of the younger churches call our own certainties into question. Of course, a theology is not true just because it comes from Buenos Aires or Jakarta. But we cannot faithfully discharge our missionary responsibility to our own people unless we are willing to listen for what the living God says to us through his servants in other cultures. We need all the saints, and the foreign missionary is not a temporary but an abiding necessity for the life of the church, provided always that the movement of missionaries is multidirectional, all churches both sending and receiving. The word of God is to be spoken in every tongue, but it can never be domesticated in any. The contemporary campaign of abuse directed against the World Council of Churches is certainly predictable and perhaps even to be welcomed as a sign that the sharp sword of the word of God is piercing our complacence and challenging the comfortable syncretism in which our Western Christianity has been living for so long.

6. The sixth requirement I would suggest for a missionary encounter with our culture is simply the courage to hold and to proclaim a belief that cannot be proved to be true in terms of the axioms of our society. This may sound simplistic, but it is not. Our modern scientific culture has pursued the ideal of a completely impersonal knowledge of a world of so-called facts that are simply there, that cannot be doubted by rational minds, and that constitute the real world as contrasted with the opinions, desires, hopes, and fears of human beings, a world in which the words *purpose* and *value* have no meaning. This whole way of trying to understand the totality of human experience rests on beliefs that are simply not questioned. For every attempt to understand and cope with experience must rest on some such belief. Every such belief is, of course, open to critical question, but no criticism is possible except by relying on other beliefs that are—in the act of criticizing—exempt from criticism.[7] All understanding of reality involves a commitment, a venture of faith. No belief system can be faulted by the fact that it rests on unproved assumptions; what can and must be faulted is the blindness of its proponents to the fact that this is so.

The gospel is not a set of beliefs that arise, or could arise, from empirical observation of the whole human experience. It is the announcement of a name and a fact that offer the starting point for a new and life-long enterprise of understanding and coping with experience. It is a new starting point. To accept it means a new beginning, a radical conversion. We cannot side-step that necessity. It has always been the case that to believe means to be turned around to face in a different direction, to be a dissenter, to go against the stream. The church needs to be very humble in acknowledging that it is itself only a learner, and it needs to pay heed to all the variety of

7. See M. Polanyi, *Personal Knowledge,* pp. 269-94.

human experience in order to learn in practice what it means that Jesus is the King and Head of the human race. But the church also needs to be very bold in bearing witness to him as the one who alone is that King and Head. For the demonstration, the proof, we have to wait for the end. Until then, we have to be bold and steadfast in our witness and patient in our hope. For "we are partakers of Christ if we hold our first confidence firm to the end" (Heb. 3:14).

7. There is one thing more that must be said. This humble boldness and this expectant patience are not the product of some kind of human heroism. They are the spontaneous overflow of a community of praise. They are the radiance of a supernatural reality. That reality is, first of all, the reality of God, the superabundant richness of the being of the Triune God, in whom love is forever given and forever enjoyed in an ever-new exchange. It is secondly the overflow of that love through the presence of the Spirit of God in the life of the community that lives by faith in Christ. It is said of this superabundant glory that it has been given to believers in order that they may be recognizable as a community where the love of God is actually tested and known (John 17:20-23). This is what makes the church a place of joy, of praise, of surprises, and of laughter—a place where there is a foretaste of the endless surprises of heaven.

In my own experience I have been touched by the evidence of two very different communities of faith into which men and women are being drawn out of the grey wastelands of a secularized and disenchanted world: the Pentecostals and the Russian Orthodox. Different as they are from one another, they have this in common: their life is centered in the action of praise—praise that is literally "out of this world" and is by that very fact able to speak to this world. Where this is present, the radiance of that supernatural reality is enough to draw men and women into its circle.

I write these words at the season of Easter, the event that is the despair of a certain kind of rationalism but the starting point for a new rationality. The event of the resurrection, the empty tomb, and the risen Lord breaks every mold that would imprison God in the rationalism of a fallen world. But it is the starting point for a new kind of rationality, for the possibility of living hopefully in a world without hope, for the perpetual praise of God who not only creates order out of chaos but also breaks through fixed orders to create ever-new situations of surprise and joy.

> When the Lord restored the fortunes of Zion,
>   we were like those who dream.
> Then our mouth was filled with laughter
>   and our tongue with shouts of joy;
> Then they said among the nations,
>   "The Lord has done great things for them."
> The Lord has done great things for us;
>   we are glad.
>
> *(Psalm 126:1-3)*

The church's witness among the nations is at heart the overflow of a gift. The boldness and the expectancy are the marks of those who have been surprised by joy and know that there are still surprises to come, because God is great.

Select Bibliography

Arendt, Hannah. *On Revolution*. New York: Viking, 1963.

Augustine, Aurelius, St. *The City of God*. Translated by G. E. McCracken. 7 vols. Cambridge: Harvard University Press, 1960–1968.

Barth, Karl. *Church Dogmatics*. Edited by G. W. Bromiley and T. F. Torrance. Edinburgh: T. & T. Clark, 1956–1977.

Becker, Carl L. *The Heavenly City of the Eighteenth Century Philosophers*. New Haven: Yale University Press, 1932.

Berger, Peter L. *The Heretical Imperative: Contemporary Possibilities of Religious Affirmation*. Garden City, NY: Anchor Press, 1979.

Brown, Peter R. L. *Augustine of Hippo: A Biography*. Berkeley and Los Angeles: University of California Press, 1967.

Bultmann, Rudolf K. *Faith and Understanding*. Translated by Louise Pettibone Smith. New York: Harper & Row, 1969.

Caird, G. B. *The Language and Imagery of the Bible*. Philadelphia: Westminster Press, 1980.

Cohn, Norman. *The Pursuit of the Millennium: Revolutionary Millenarians and Mystical Anarchists of the Middle Ages*. London and New York: Oxford University Press, 1970.

Dooyeweerd, Herman. *Roots of Western Culture: Pagan, Secular, and Christian Options*. Beaver Falls, PA: Radix Books, 1979.

Eliot, T. S. *Idea of a Christian Society*. New York: Harcourt, Brace and Co., 1940.

Frei, Hans. *The Eclipse of the Biblical Narrative: A Study in Eighteenth- and Nineteenth-Century Hermeneutics*. New Haven: Yale University Press, 1974.

Gilkey, Langdon. *How the Church Can Minister to the World Without Losing Itself*. New York: Harper & Row, 1964.

Habgood, John. *Church and Nation in a Secular Age*. London: Darton, Longman & Todd, 1983.

Hardy, Daniel W. and David F. Ford. *Jubilate: Theology in Praise*. London: Darton, Longman & Todd, 1984.

Ignatieff, Michael. *The Needs of Strangers*. New York: Viking, 1985.

Ionescu, Ghita. *Politics and the Pursuit of Happiness*. London and New York: Longman, 1984.

Jaki, Stanley. *The Road of Science and the Ways to God*. Chicago: University of Chicago Press, 1978.

Kelsey, David H. *The Uses of Scripture in Recent Theology*. Philadelphia: Fortress Press, 1975.

Luckman, Thomas. *The Invisible Religion: The Problem of Religion in Modern Society*. New York: Macmillan, 1967.

MacIntyre, Alasdair. *After Virtue*. London: Duckworth, 1981.

Maritain, Jacques. *True Humanism*. New York: Charles Scrib-

152

ner's Sons, 1938.

Munby, Arthur N. *The Idea of a Secular Society and Its Significance for Christians.* London and New York: Oxford University Press, 1963.

Nineham, Dennis E. *The Use and Abuse of the Bible.* New York: Barnes and Noble, 1976.

Novak, Michael. *The Spirit of Democratic Capitalism.* New York: Simon & Schuster, 1982.

Peacocke, A. R. *Creation and the World of Science.* London and New York: Oxford University Press, 1979.

Plant, Raymond, et al. *Political Philosophy and Social Welfare: Essays on the Normative Basis of Welfare Provision.* London: Routledge and Kegan Paul, 1980.

Polanyi, Michael. *Personal Knowledge: Towards a Post-Critical Philosophy.* Chicago: University of Chicago Press, 1958.

Richey, Russell E., ed. *Denominationalism.* Nashville: Abingdon, 1977.

Schleiermacher, Friedrich. *The Christian Faith.* Translated by H. R. Mackintosh and J. S. Stewart. Philadelphia: Fortress Press, 1977.

Stuhlmacher, Peter. *Historical Criticism and Theological Interpretation of Scripture.* Translated by Roy A. Harrisville. Philadelphia: Fortress Press, 1977.

Tawney, Richard H. *Religion and the Rise of Capitalism.* New York: Harcourt, Brace and Co., 1926.

Teilhard de Chardin, Pierre. *The Divine Milieu.* New York: Harper & Row, 1960.

Thorpe, William H. *Purpose in a World of Chance: A Biologist's View.* London and New York: Oxford University Press, 1978.

Zaehner, R. C. *Mysticism: Sacred and Profane.* London and New York: Oxford University Press, 1961.

Index

Adaptation (of the gospel), 2
Apocalyptic expectation, 98-99, 105-6
Arendt, Hannah, 30, 34
Atheism, 65, 67, 106
Augustine of Hippo, 102-5, 133-34

Baillie, John, 131
Barth, Karl, 11
Becker, Carl, 106
Berger, Peter, 10-17
Bible: as book of the believing community, 55-58; concepts or principles extracted from, 47-48, critical study of, 42, 43, 46-47; discontinuity between human wisdom and biblical revelation ("paradigm shift"), 51-54, 62, 64; doctrine of the church, 145; on freedom, 141; fundamentalism, 45-46; gulf between Bible world and ours, 47; hermeneutical circle, 51-54, 56, 58; and history, 60-63; on human nature, 97-98, 118-119; on politics, 97-99, 125-28; as professional property of scholars, 142; "rendering" God, 59-61; salvation history, 48, 61; summons to authentic existence, 48-50; Torah, 97-98, 99; and tradition, 58; understood in terms of scientific world-view, 45, 55; as word of God, 10
Biology, modern, 73-75, 91-92
Bosch, David, 132
Bultmann, Rudolf, 11-12, 48-50
Bureaucracy, 32-33

Calvin, John, 106-7
Calvinism, 108
Capitalism: atheist, 106; as cancer in society, 114; ideological warfare with Marxism, 110-11; Novak on, 111-14; and Puritan Calvinism, 108; Reformers and rise of, 106-7; unrestrained, 121-22
Capra, Fritjof, 39
Christendom, 101, 105, 106, 124, 128-29

Christian Faith, The (Schleiermacher), 44
Christian state, 130-31, 137, 140
Church: in Augustine's *City of God,* 102-5; biblical doctrine of, 145; birth of, 99; and Christendom, 101, 105, 106, 124, 128-29; as community of praise, 149; as community in the Bible, 55-58; and Constantine, 100-101; denominationalism of, 144-46; desacralized, 42-43; distinction of church and state, 130; and ecumenical movement, 146, 147; and imperial Rome, 99-100; and protest movements, 124-25; and society, 95, 99-102, 103-8, 115, 117, 124-50; testimony of, 88-91, 94, 115, 117, 123, 124-25, 129, 148-50; and World Council of Churches, 147-48
City of God, The (Augustine), 102-5
Cohn, Norman, 105
Constantine, Emperor, 100-101
Contextualization, 2
Conversion, 148
Corpus Christianum. See Christendom
Cosmology, 69-70, 72-73, 93
Crick, F. H. C., 73-74
Critical study of the Bible, 42, 43, 46-47
Cross of Christ, 90-91, 99, 123, 125-27, 136
Culture: definition of, 3; influence on presentation of gospel, 4; and Jesus, 8-9, 146. *See also* Modern Western culture

Death, 135-36
"Declericalized" theology, 141-44
Denominationalism, 144-46
Dialogue, missionary, 139-40, 147
Dietrich, Suzanne de, 142
Dikaiosune, 132-33
Division of labor, 29-30
Dooyeweerd, Hermann, 131, 143

Eastern religions: compatibility with scientific world-view, 39-40; in British schools, 39

Economics: of capitalism, 30-31, 106-8, 110, 111-14, 121-22; division of labor, 29-30; ever-increasing production, 110, 114; market economy, origins of, 30-31; Marxism, 106, 110; modern science of, 108-9; no business of church, 95-96; Novak's views on, 111-14; part of Christian ethics, 106-8; and the Reformers, 106-7

Ecumenical Institute, Bossey, 142

Ecumenical movement, 146, 147

Education, 38-39, 140

Eliot, T. S., 131

Enlightenment: doctrine of progress, 28-29, 134-35; genesis of modern culture, 22-23; human rights, 26-27; nation-state, 27; reason, 25; science, 24-25

Equality, 118-22

Eschatology, 134-37

"Facts" (folk-concept): denied by practices of science, 77; over against beliefs, 76-77; over against values, 16-19, 35-39, 78

Feuerbach, Ludwig, 45

Ford, David, 93

Freedom, 118-22, 137-41

Frei, Hans, 59

Fundamentalism, 45-46

Ghazali, al-, 12

Gibbon, Edward, 138

Gilkey, Langdon, 46, 106

Gladstone, W. E., 20, 131-32

God: as Creator and Sustainer of the universe, 88-89; as Holy Spirit, 127-28, 149; Incarnation, 89-90; kingdom (kingship, reign) of, 98-99, 126-28, 134; knowledge of, 88, 89-90; as Lord of history, 60-63; "rendered" in the Bible, 59-61; Triune, 89-90, 149

Gospel: adaptation, 2; cannot be proved true, 148; communication to Hellenistic world, 53; contextualization of, 2; cross-cultural communication of, 4-9; culturally conditioned, 4; definition of, 3-4; false, 132-33; indigenization of, 2; as part of Western culture, 43-44, 101; resisted by modern Western culture, 3. See also Bible; Church

Gospel according to John, 53

Hardy, Daniel, 93

Heretical Imperative, The (Berger), 10-17

Hermeneutical circle, 51-54, 56, 58

Hertz, Karl, 144

History, 60-63, 103

Hocking, W. E., 2

Holy Spirit, 127-28

Holy Trinity, 89-90, 149

Hudson, Winthrop, 144

Human nature: and the Bible, 97-98, 118-19; fulfilled in relationships, 118-19, 122; Indian and Greek thought in, 96

Human rights, 26-27, 120-21

Incarnation, 89-90

Indigenization, 2

Ionescu, Ghita, 117

Islamic society, 115-16

Jesus: and the Cross, 90-91, 99, 125-27, 136; culturally conditioned presentations of, 8-9, 146; Incarnation of, 89-90; message of, 98-99; and power, 125-27; resurrection of, 62-63, 90-91, 99, 127, 136, 150; sonship of, 89-90, 126

Johannine writings, 6, 53

Justice: in Augustine's City of God, 104-5; dikaiosune, 132-33

Kingdom (kingship, reign) of God, 98-99, 126-28, 134

Knowledge: "the facts" of, 76; of God, 88-90; Laplace's view of, 65; and learning, 79-80; of other persons, 84-88, 89; reciprocity of, 84-85, 89-90; significant patterns of, 80-81;

tacit, 80; understanding in terms of purpose, 81-83
Kraemer, Hendrik, 142
Kuhn, Thomas, 52
Kuyper, Abraham, 143

Labor, division of, 29-30
Laplace, Pierre-Simon, Marquis de, 65, 80
Lay theology, 141-44
Love, 104-5
Luckman, Thomas, 145
Luther, Martin, 106-7

MacIntyre, Alasdair, 36-37, 76-77, 133-34
Maritain, Jacques, 113, 131
Market economy, 30-31
Marxism, 106, 110
Mead, Sidney, 144
Mechanical models: in science, 73-75, in society, 66
Millenarian movements, 105-6
Missionaries, missions: adaptation of, 2; attacks on public life of culture, 95; author's experience of, 1, 21; contextualization of, 2; cross-cultural communication of the gospel, 7-9, 42; dialogue of, 139-40; indigenization, 2; missionary encounter with modern Western culture, 124-50; multi-directional, 147
Modern Western culture: atheism in, 65, 67, 106; bureaucracy of, 32-33; confidence in scientific world-view, 16-18, 54-55, 65-68; division of labor in, 29-30; dominance of, 40; education in, 38-39; market economy of, 30-31; mechanically organized, 66; missionary encounter with, 124-50; origins in the Enlightenment, 22-29; paganism in, 20; plausibility structure of, 10-11, 13-15, 17-18, 54, 58, 62-63; pluralism of, 15-17; separation of "facts" and values or beliefs, 16-18, 35-39, 76-77, 78; separation of

private and public life, 18-19, 31, 35-39; teleology of, 24, 34-35, 37-38; urbanization of, 32
"Moral Majority." *See* "Religious Right"
Munby, Arthur, 131

Nation-state, 27
Needs, 119-21
Newton, Isaac, 24
Niebuhr, Richard, 1, 144
Nineham, Dennis, 47
Novak, Michael, 111-14

Paganism, 20
Paradigm shift, 52, 64
Paul: principalities and powers, 126, 128; speech before Agrippa, 5
Petty, Sir William, 109
Physics, modern, 67-70, 72, 92-93
Plant, Raymond, 120
Plausibility structures, 10-11, 13-15, 17-18, 54, 58, 62-63
Pluralism, 15-17
Polanyi, M., 65, 80
Politics: and the Bible, 97-99, 125-28; and the church, 95-96, 99-102, 115, 117, 124-41; distinction of church and state, 130; and eschatology, 136-37; capitalism, 106-8, 110, 111-14, 121-2; Ionescu's definition of, 117; and Islam, 115-16; Marxism, 106, 110; "Religious Right," 116-17; socialism, 114
Power (political): God's gift of, 129-30; in New Testament, 125-28
Private life. *See* Public life
Progress, doctrine of, 28-29, 134-35
Protest movements, 124-25
Public life as separate from private life, 18-19, 31, 35-39
Purpose: absence from Eastern religions, 39; in animal world, 91-92; eliminated from scientific world-view, 24, 34-35, 38; persistence of concept of, 35, 37, 77-78, 81-83

Reason, 25
Reign of God. *See* Kingdom of God
Relationships, 118-19, 122
Religion: and science, 66-67. *See also* Bible; Church; Gospel; Religious experience
Religious experience: Berger's views on, 12-13, 15, 17; as center of unity for world religions, 40-41; Schleiermacher's views on, 44
"Religious Right," 116-17
Resurrection of Jesus, 62-63, 90, 99, 127, 136, 150
Rights, human, 26-27, 120-21
Roman Empire, 99-101

Salvation history, 48, 61
Schleiermacher, F., 12, 44
Science: and cosmology, 69-70, 72-73; development depends on view of universe as rational and contingent, 70-72; mechanical models of, 73-75; modern biology, 73-75, 91-92; modern physics, 68-70, 72, 92-93; purpose in scientific activity, 77; and religion, 66-67; significant patterns of, 80-81; social sciences, 75, 78. *See also* Scientific world-view
Scientific world-view: essential features of, 67-68; "facts," 16-17, 76-77; modern Western confidence in, 16-18, 54-55, 65-68; origins of, 24-25; as plausibility structure, 18, 54, 58, 62-63; scientific method applied to Bible, 42, 43, 45, 55; scientific method applied to truth-claims of religions, 17-18
Scripture. *See* Bible
Secular state, 130, 131-32
Social sciences, 75, 78; economics, 29-31, 95-96, 106-14; politics, 95-96, 99-102

Socialism, 114, 118, 119-21
Society: in Augustine's *City of God,* 102-5; biblical view of, 97-99, 125-28; capitalist, 106-8, 110, 111-14, 121-22; and Christendom, 101, 105, 106, 128-29; Christian state, 130-31, 140; and church, 95-96, 99-102, 103-8, 115, 117, 124-50; division of labor, 29-30; economic laws of, 108-10; Islamic, 115-16; Marxist, 106, 110; millenarian revolts in, 105-6; Reformers' views of, 106-7; secular state, 130, 131-32; socialism, 114; welfare state, 119-21
"Sphere sovereignty," 143-44
Spirit of Democratic Capitalism, The (Novak), 111-14
State: Christian, 130-31, 137, 140; distinct from church, 130; secular, 130, 131-32. *See also* Politics; Society
Stuhlmacher, P., 57

Tawney, R. H., 106, 108
Teilhard de Chardin, Pierre, 141-42
Teleology. *See* Purpose
Theology: and cosmology, 69-70, 93; "declericalized" (lay), 141-44. *See also* Bible; Gospel; Religion; Religious experience
Tillich, Paul, 1
Tolerance, 137-40
Tradition, 58
Trinity, Holy, 89-90, 149

Values over against "facts," 16-19, 35-39
Visser 't Hooft, W. A., 142

Wants, 119-21
Warfield, Benjamin, 46
Welfare state, 119-21
World Council of Churches, 147-48